MW00981664

<u>Inspired me...</u>

"When You're Not You" inspired me to recommit to my recovery. Even my husband is reading it, relating and understanding me now!

- Catherine Marney, Vancouver BC

<u>All men need to read this!</u>

All men need to read this book, and women too.

- Eileen Roth, North Vancouver, BC

<u>...it really says it all!</u>

This is the first recovery book that really says it all. It clearly shows the path and describes the work.

- Barbara Glauser, Duncan, BC

<u>...challenged, yet rewarded!</u>

"When You're Not You" led me into my deepest concealed emotions where I discovered that my fears were mere illusions. I emerged, feeling at ease with myself.

- Olga Takacs, artist, Duncan, BC
www.famousartreproductions.com

When You're Not You

A Personal Journey Through Addictions,
Childhood Abuse and Codependency

Ted McIntyre and Kelly Dame

© Copyright 2005 Ted McIntyre and Kelly Dame.
All rights reserved. No part of this publication may be reproduced, stored in a retrieval system, or transmitted, in any form or by any means, electronic, mechanical, photocopying, recording, or otherwise, without the written prior permission of the author.

Note for Librarians: A cataloguing record for this book is available from Library and Archives Canada at www.collectionscanada.ca/amicus/index-e.html
ISBN 1-4120-6624-7

Printed in Victoria, BC, Canada. Printed on paper with minimum 30% recycled fibre. Trafford's print shop runs on "green energy" from solar, wind and other environmentally-friendly power sources.

PUBLISHING™
Offices in Canada, USA, Ireland and UK
This book was published *on-demand* in cooperation with Trafford Publishing. On-demand publishing is a unique process and service of making a book available for retail sale to the public taking advantage of on-demand manufacturing and Internet marketing. On-demand publishing includes promotions, retail sales, manufacturing, order fulfilment, accounting and collecting royalties on behalf of the author.

Book sales for North America and international:
Trafford Publishing, 6E–2333 Government St.,
Victoria, BC v8t 4p4 CANADA
phone 250 383 6864 (toll-free 1 888 232 4444)
fax 250 383 6804; email to orders@trafford.com
Book sales in Europe:
Trafford Publishing (uk) Limited, 9 Park End Street, 2nd Floor
Oxford, UK oxi 1hh UNITED KINGDOM
phone 44 (0)1865 722 113 (local rate 0845 230 9601)
facsimile 44 (0)1865 722 868; info.uk@trafford.com
Order online at:
trafford.com/05-1535

10 9 8 7 6 5 4 3

Dedication

We dedicate this book to every person who, for whatever reason, has made the decision to enter a journey of recovery and hopes to effect major changes in their life. We honor your courage and we celebrate your commitment.

Best Wishes,
Kelly and Ted.

Hi Margarita

It's great talking to you. It's nice to meet somebody in the same business. You get it!

Ted. Kelly

5

Children who grow up in alcoholic or dysfunctional families
learn three basic rules:
Don't talk.
Don't trust.
Don't feel.

Paraphrased from *"Adult Children of Alcoholics"*
Janet Geringer Woititz

Table of Contents

Acknowledgements

Our parents: May and Bill McIntyre and Ann Martin and Bob Dame.

Friends and family: Greg, Robin, Carly; Emma, Gina, Dale and Brittany; Olga, Louis, Karen, Michael and Adrienne; Barbara, Emery, Lindsay, Carman and Calen; Eileen; Catherine, Craig and Brendan; John and Doris; Irene and Natalie.

Counselors and therapists: Father Larry Mackey, Patricia Spears, Paul Kaufman, John Arnold and Deborah Abood.

Book support: Barbara, Eileen, Catherine, Olga and Lisa for designing the book cover.

In loving memory of our sister-in-law Chris.

Cover art by August Macke 1914.

Introduction

When my wife, Kelly, and I decided to collaborate on a book it struck a chord in us in some deep place that seemed both ancient, yet familiar. The ensuing energy surged through our bodies, awakening our excitement and passion, causing a flood of ideas and a sense of purpose. Hope was renewed. Then it ebbed and was gone.

The decision to collaborate wasn't the result of logical thinking - it was more along the lines of inspiration. We had been pleading with our higher power and guides to show us the next step on the path of our spiritual journey and we didn't seem to be getting the answers.

We had just completed seven years of front line work with trauma-based fetal alcohol children and we were doing everything we could to escape the shadow of burnout that had been stalking our Jeep around the entire coast of Mexico. The dark cloud that we towed from BC to California, through the Mojave Dessert to the Grand Canyon, and from Sonora State south to Quintana Roo, cast a shadow on our spiritual receptivity and it blocked the enjoyment of our experience.

We knew that we needed time to heal. We were using the small sum from my mother's estate, not as originally planned to purchase a larger home to expand our business, but to desperately save our health and our marriage.

Beaches and sun have always been the tonic for both of us, thus the Mexican adventure, a twenty two thousand kilometer odyssey that, in retrospect, reconnected us to ourselves and redefined how we were in relation to purpose.

Neither of us speaks Spanish, so we decided to purchase a small phrase book. The only other significant thing we brought was a brown paper lunch bag that contained a new set of angel cards. One of our friends back home said something we liked so we wrote it on the bag: "Relax, take care of yourself and the answers will come".

We decided to spend one month in Playa del Carmen on the Caribbean coast. The white sand and the turquoise water were the goal we were drawn to. We ate healthy, walked the beach and got decadently brown, yet there was still something missing.

Kelly and I collectively have about thirty years of recovery and are constantly aspiring for growth. We have also done a lot of therapy and have a good sense of transition, loss and the grieving process. We knew that our work as therapeutic interventionists was coming to an end. It depleted us. We needed to find something that would feed us on all levels.

On our journey we have taken what we liked from a number of sources and we have adapted our personal program to be an eclectic potpourri. One of our basic offerings in meditation is to ask that our work serve as a vehicle to help people. We chose a prayer from the Course in Miracles:

What would you have me do?
Where would you have me go?
What would you have me say, and to whom?

And of course, the basic twelve step tenet:

"Thy will, not mine, be done."

Thoughts of returning home with no job, no money and worst of all no goal took its toll on us. Fear began to stalk us, too. In despair and frustration we implored our guides to show us our next step. There was no voice, no sign, no indication that we were being heard. What were we doing wrong? Why weren't we getting it?

While walking the beach at Playa del Carmen the inspiration came, the energy and the flow of ideas followed. It was raw power and we decided that there were possibly several books in us, one about working with kids, one on recovery, another in developing intimacy in recovery and one on marriage in recovery! It felt so good to have excitement about something! We envisioned the perfect place to write - quiet, peaceful and near water.

Instead of staying for the six months as intended, we knew it was time to return home. The knowingness transcended the mere fact that we were running out of money. September 11, 2001 saw us in El Paso, Texas and we emotionally limped home from there, soothed only by the natural beauty of New Mexico and the Colorado mountains, where we stood in snow on the pass into Aspen. Next Utah, Idaho, Washington, Vancouver, BC and then back home to Vancouver Island. We were numb again and 911 was no longer exclusively a telephone number for emergency services. We couldn't make any major decisions so we continued to rent out our townhouse and furniture for a year and, at the very least, had our mortgage covered.

We had the option of renting my father-in-law's furnished cabin on the lake. No one had responded to his ad and it was available. No phone, small town, peace and quiet. The other option was shared accommodation in the city: stress, high costs and starting over.

The duel with fear was getting fiercer and I found myself slipping back into an old place, suicidal thinking. We were now living on our credit line and the only work looked like reopening a new care home back on the mainland or taking upgrading to become certified therapists. There was no energy here, even though we took the beginning moves and interviewed a facility offering addiction-counseling courses.

We continued to use prayer and meditation and we decided to feng shui the cabin. Immediately things began to happen. Surprise! Surprise!

The first message came from Melody Beattie's daily meditation book for October 31. Kelly got it right away and I didn't, but when she read it in her voice the message hit home.

"Our task is to allow ourselves to come into harmony with our source. Our task is to believe in and look to our true source. Our task is to release fear, negative thinking, limitations and short supply thinking." It gave me something to focus on when I awoke in the middle of the night and encountered the old thinking that spirals me into despair and hopelessness (a road I no longer want to travel).

The second gift came a few days later, as we were drinking our morning tea, looking at the lake, reading our meditation book and choosing our daily angel card. We both thought about writing the book again. Here we were, a quiet cabin on a beautifully peaceful portion of the lake, which we were renting for an absurdly low monthly payment - HELLO!! It was everything we had asked for. The energy returned. It was the total transformational variety and we knew that we had once again reconnected with source and that source was within us. We shook hands on it and made the commitment.

The third significant message came through Karen Rauch Carter's Feng Shui book *Move your Stuff, Change your Life*. Something we have heard in many ways before "energy follows thought, so wherever intention goes, the energy flows." We knew then that we could be writers because that was our intention and we certainly had energy around it. It was enough to begin and led us to our next step, as Dr. Phil says: "You've got to name it to claim it." And that really worked well for Kelly, who loves Oprah, loves Dr. Phil and who loves to use shock value to shake up people's belief systems. She immediately began informing friends and family that we were now writers. In her words, "first they closed down a successful agency, then they went to Mexico for six months and spent all their savings, and now they are writing a book and living on their credit line."

We believe that there are no mistakes and that we are exactly where we are supposed to be. We have asked for guidance and have asked for messages and to offer inspiration. If something in this book touches you our work will have been done.

On another level, this book is essential to our spiritual unfolding, getting unstuck and evolving our sense of self-actualization. It was imperative for both of us to access our creativity, to claim and to begin to develop our talents - without this vehicle we would have withered and died.

Thanks also to Iyanla, who offered this pearl:

"Be willing to let it all go for the commitment to have it all."

Worst case scenario - we sell our cars and our Jeep, our townhouse, our furniture and our paintings and we start over.

Seventeen years ago I was down and out. Twelve years ago everything I owned was in my car. Five years ago we purchased a home and began to fill it with stuff. It's just stuff (and stuff and jobs are not our Source).

This book is about recovery. It is about the movement from powerlessness, victimhood, addictions, codependency, ineffectual belief systems, desperation, despondency, hopelessness and despair to claiming power, accountability, joy, success and hope for the future. Shift happens!

This book is also about spirituality, changing belief systems, forming healthy relationships, and connecting with and believing in a higher power.

Finally, it is about examining how we are in relationship to the people and events in our daily lives, living in the present, making healthy choices, creating who we are and achieving all our wants and needs. Enjoy the journey.

Love,

Kelly and Ted.

PART ONE

LEARNING TO TALK

Chapter One

Hitting Bottom

*A*s I sit here at my honey-red country pine table looking out the window *at the beauty of our first snow, I am awed. Three inches of a brilliant, new blanket contrasts with the stark, cold gray of the lake. Somehow I don't mind that the power is out. The only heat comes from our woodstove working overtime in the corner. It's doing double duty heating leftovers and warming our water for tea. I am grateful for all that I have.*

It's almost the end of November and the season invites me inward like an insect burrowing underground for over-wintering. Conversely, I am nearly compelled to throw open the door and walk naked, out into the cold – the cold of a remembered prairie winter in 1984, eighteen years ago.

It was February or March. I had been newly hired as course superintendent at a small town golf course just south of Edmonton, Alberta. There were huge drifts of snow. The cold foreshadowed fear and death. I couldn't risk getting stopped on the road because I had lost my license for impaired driving. Although I was driving an old beater of an Oldsmobile, I was forced to rely on cruise control to regulate my speed and avoid traffic tickets. I chuckled as I remembered my friend Pots wearing a sailor's hat while navigating traffic in his convertible Pontiac Parisienne. He would set his cruise control and drive that big boat all over Calgary.

On an average day I was up at four-thirty and home from work by three-thirty P.M.. Then a half a dozen reefers fortified with hash oil and a flat (24 cans) of Olympia beer would launch me out of my head. I'd be nameless, bouncing off the walls, by early evening. Then I'd lurch down the hall to my room where I would pass out until morning.

During the day, I drank a dozen or more cups of coffee, each with up to five heaping teaspoons of sugar, and smoked two large packs of cigarettes (25 per pack). On weekends, I worked half days so that I could be home by eleven a.m. to begin my ritual early. That expanded the time for me to inhale my two flats of beer and four packs of smokes. Simultaneously, I sipped on Remy Martin and nursed scotch and water out of a small, thick-walled flowerpot that wouldn't break when it invariably slipped out of my hand and hit the floor. I had trained that pot to bounce once or twice before my sluggish reflexes told me to scoop it up.

Now don't get me wrong. I hadn't always drank this much – only the previous seven years. Prior to that I was out and about, socializing in the bars with anyone who would tolerate me. I thought I was a social butterfly but was more likely a drunken bar fly. People saw me as a social climbing namedropper who aspired to be a jock. My bingeing began when I left home at the age of eighteen to attend university. It persisted for over seventeen years except for nine months that I spent in the arctic. During that period, I had survived on pot and Valium.

I had attended Notre Dame University in the mountain town of Nelson, BC. That had been a last-minute choice after the two major universities in British Columbia had denied me entry. In my final year of high school I had transferred from Quebec and my transcripts and prerequisites were not up to British Columbia standards. Notre Dame University was advertising space available. Urged by my mom, I phoned Notre Dame on a Friday. On Saturday my little red Datsun was loaded and I was on my way to Nelson.

University quickly became another disappointment. Instead of attending classes, I excelled in intramural sports and became a late evening regular in the town pubs. The school was the only one in Canada that had scholarships for sports. It boasted members of Canada's National Ski Team. Hockey players that had been attracted from major junior and minor pro ranks played on the local senior hockey team. I was neither a ranked skier nor a skilled hockey competitor, but I could drink with the best of them. I never missed an opportunity to go into town to the pubs.

The school was small, about six to eight hundred students in each year. Everyone, with the exception of married students, lived in residence. There was a chapel on campus and a curious collection of academics on staff that included many clergy.

Several factors enriched the local color and created an unusual social ambiance. Nelson and the Slocan Valley boasted a large Dukabor population. This Russian peasant group clashed with the young American draft dodgers who were resisting the Vietnam war. The draft dodgers investigated rural redevelopment by setting up elaborate communes. Others attended the arts school. It was the era of Woodstock, long hair, acid and heavy rock. The social ambiance was exciting; it was "far out, man." Students came from all over the world, Europe, the Middle East, Africa, South America, Asia, the United States and Canada. Everyone came together with a sense of belonging and family. The skier, Nancy Green, had just won Olympic Gold and the school and Canadians felt proud.

If you chose to participate in getting an education, there were classes, reading, term papers, midterms, lectures and uninspiring seminars. Comprehensive examinations loomed if you successfully maneuvered the registrar's shuffle and threatened to graduate.

My choice came easily. For four years I lived outrageously under the mistaken impression that negative attention equaled popularity; I would do just about anything to attract attention. I cut classes and dropped courses, and turned down an offer from the head of the English department to write seriously. I had adopted the Epicurean philosophy of "eat, drink and be merry for tomorrow you may die." I was arrested twice for drunken college pranks.

By my fourth year at Notre Dame, I succeeded in making the varsity hockey team. However, my constant carousing earned me more bench time than ice time. My other contribution to the school was organizing an alumni ski race that was well attended.

After my fourth year, I was kicked out of university. Curiously, I didn't discover this fact until several years later when I returned for one more attempt to finish. My goal while in university the first time was to make it to thirty without committing to a career. I regarded myself as a free spirit who was experimenting with an alternative life style.

Employment was almost too easy to find, like the summer jobs in the BC sawmill or the Manitoba nickel mine. I obtained a position as powerhouse operator in a silver mine in the Northwest Territories. I flew into the camp after a weeklong "road trip" to Calgary and Edmonton. In withdrawal, I was shaking badly enough to catch the eye of the knowing hard-rock veterans. It was a day camp and I stayed sober, but once back in town I quickly managed to piss my summer earnings down the drain.

I was lured to Vancouver to pursue professional sales where I was a flash-in-the-pan for eight months. The company made the mistake of offering me a week's holiday. I journeyed to Nelson to enjoy the summer sun. I had been lonely in the city and it was great to be back with friends. I attended a wedding and spent a lot of time in the pub. To say the least, I was over-served and caught by the dreaded bar magnet. In my stupor, I was enticed by local work opportunities in the school system. I phoned my boss in Vancouver and resigned my sales position.

My life seemed full. I taught both junior and senior high school on a substitute basis. This was before the advent of the teacher's union when more than two years of post secondary education would be required for substitute teachers. I managed a maintenance level of evening drinking and weekend bingeing.

From the time the snow came in December, I skied Monday to Friday, until March when I returned to teaching. School had always been easy for me when I focused. I preferred teaching math, French and physical education. On more than one occasion I landed full time employment until the end of the school year.

My summers were filled with water skiing, beaching and guzzling beer. I knew this couldn't last forever. It didn't. One winter in my late twenties I hurt myself skiing. I had smoked a reefer on the lift line with my buddy. We let out as much board as we could handle, intending to run the downhill course the day after the world cup hopefuls had moved on to the Colorado races. On a section known as Indian Flats near the bottom of the course, I caught an edge and went over the front of my skis. I had been skiing for years and had taken a lot of falls with minor injuries. This time I knew I was hurt. My pelvis was thrown out of alignment.

To make matters worse, my unemployment benefits were terminated when I was injured. I tried to collect welfare but instead the agency assigned me to work with youth. I couldn't do that because I couldn't stay straight.

I was always buzzed and vibrating too much to spend time in public. I was forced to ask my parents who lived in Vancouver if I could stay with them while I healed. We didn't particularly get along. I hadn't seen them for years and asking them for sanctuary now was tense. They consented to my staying with them temporarily.

I put the drug use to rest. The local golf pro took my ski equipment in trade for a set of clubs and I began a new chapter in my illustrious life. I had little natural ability at golf but hard work and persistence got me to the point where I broke a hundred, then ninety.

Having had their fill of my convalescence, my parents were ready for me to be away again. I had planned to hit the road to find construction work in northern Alberta when fate intervened. My great aunt passed away, appointing me executor to her will.

I worked a deal with my great aunt's lawyer who had his eye on the French inlaid coffee table that was said to have come from the Wells-Fargo estate. In exchange for acquiring this antique, the lawyer paid me a custodian's salary to caretake the property while the estate was in probate. I isolated myself in that house and, for the first time as an adult, I began to drink alone. I mixed alcohol with pot and handpicked psychedelic mushrooms.

While living in isolation at my great aunt's home, I had my first untreated breakdown. The symptoms manifested in my spending the winter watching TV game shows. I had frenzied crying spells when I would literally rip my clothes off before I passed out. I became extremely paranoid. Ultimately, I managed to quit the drugs cold turkey. The resilience of youth, combined with spring air and a return to the golf course, helped me straighten out. Feeling more myself, I decided to return to Nelson.

With approximately thirty thousand dollars that I had received from my late aunt's estate, I went back to school at Notre Dame. My new direction was to take English courses and eventually get my teaching certificate. I bought a small house in Nelson and attended classes. I did quite well until Christmas. That winter I slipped back into my old ways. Within two years the money was gone, the house was gone and I was undergoing my second breakdown.

To make matters worse I lost my job with the railroad and I was about to get canned from my new temporary job at the local golf course because the volunteer chairman of the greens committee was my ex-railroad boss.

I shared an apartment with Grayson, the course superintendent, who wasn't maintaining his hold on reality much better than I was. That winter he managed my unemployment cheques for me and administered my daily allowance of pot and alcohol. I hated the situation. I felt like a kept person who couldn't manage on his own. After surviving the winter, I knew it was time to move on. I had worn out my welcome in the town. It was too difficult to stay in Nelson when all my friends had a life: they had married, had established careers, built homes and were raising children.

On the other hand, I had only been a taker. I fancied myself as part of the town social elite because I rubbed shoulders with several NHL hockey players, ex-national ski team members and an assortment of yuppies and professionals. I acquired acquaintances that reflected power and control either from their own talents or vicariously from prominent parents. My self-esteem came from who I knew, not from who I was.

I was a promiscuous dilettante. The local discos were my hunting ground where I practiced foreplay on the dance floor as I auditioned prospective partners to take home. I had a few casual relationships but never actually had a girlfriend. My relationship was with alcohol. My purpose was to gain attention and be recognized as one of the boys.

The decision to leave Nelson was obvious; I had bottomed out there. There were no longer any doors open to me. My drug use had put me over the edge and it separated me from my former acquaintances who remained social drinkers. People were reluctant to talk to me. I was delusional and beginning to exhibit psychotic tendencies. I had that shame-based hangdog look.

Part of me died. My spirit shriveled. I could no longer be "Tundra," the self-appointed nickname that identified me to my social group. The name came from my time in the Arctic and my friends affectionately teased if brains were trees my mind would be vast tundra. The local nightclub had a drink called the TTO - the Teddy Tundra Overdrive (tequila, tia maria and ouzo). With the emergence of my dark side, I overheard the comment "Teddy Tundra, the Arctic Circle jerk." It was goodbye to Hawk and Ratso, Lifter, Groovy, Tickets, Puck and Finnigan, Cannon, Percy, Did and Foxy, Razz and Spratt. New horizons awaited me; I had farther to fall.

That spring found me in Radium, BC with my superintendent friend, working on a new golf course. I had attended mid-summer hockey games and raft races in Radium but I wasn't accepted the same way now that I wasn't hanging around with my NHL acquaintances. The drinking and drug use was escalating and the job was gone by September. Ironically, I was fired on Labour Day. I had decided that a football game in Calgary was more important than opening day for the new course and nuked my job in the process.

Landing on my feet as usual, I got a job banging nails on a new townhouse development. I quickly despised my foreman and the site superintendent. I had no experience at construction and they weren't willing or able to be my teachers.

I developed a social connection with the labourers and joined them to watch a World Series baseball game. After the game, multiple beers and a few puffs of homegrown pot, we decided to play a pick-up game of football. I ran a short pattern, caught an easy pass and attempted to make a move on my defender. I shifted to the right but my knee didn't support me. Everyone on the field heard the cartilage snap.

I was literally out of the game. After an agonizing night with no sleep, friends helped me cram my belongings in my car and pointed me in the direction of Calgary to seek the medical help of a specialist. Coincidentally, the specialist was the team doctor for the local professional football team. He drained my hugely swollen right knee and arrogantly informed me that there was nothing wrong. The next specialist, five years and much agony later, told me after my operation that I had torn the cartilage, twice.

Because I had been an "out and about" kind of guy, I knew people in Calgary and was offered a place to stay. By the springtime, I began my apprenticeship at the Calgary Country Club where I was paid the rock-bottom wage of five dollars an hour. Friends gave me free rent as I moved through the golf course hierarchy from labourer and operator to foreman and finally to assistant superintendent.

I was a legend in my own mind, a veteran performer, seasoned in my chosen avocation – drinking and drugging. The combination of harsher winters and increased drug use catapulted me into isolation and remorse. Both winters during which I attended trade school in Northern Alberta were disasters. My first year, I was kicked out of residence and moved into a room over the bar where I worked part time. I was allowed back into residence my second year and maintained a low profile quietly nursing my addictions. Spring saw me in court facing charges of non-payment of student loans.

25

Conflicts began to pop up more frequently and my boss in Calgary hinted that it was time to move on. That brings us back to that cold prairie night where this chapter began. My term as course superintendent lasted only about four months. I hated the golf course and detested my greens chairman. They liked my work but were concerned when they discovered I didn't have a driver's license and couldn't drive the golf course pickup because the insurance wouldn't cover me. Things rapidly went from bad to worse. I worked ten or twelve hours a day and then self medicated for two or three hours.

The lack of sleep and extraordinary stress combined with my substance abuse quickly rendered me psychotic. I became delusional and imagined that I was caught up in a bizarre scheme where mafia enforcers colluded with greens committee members to make a hit on me.

One morning just before I snapped, I was certain that a bomb was wired to the ignition of our old tractor. The tractor needed to be moved and I heroically turned that key fully expecting that I would be blown to bits. Another unsettling memory was lying in bed unable to sleep and hearing a train parked on a nearby siding. The engine was breathing heavy and rhythmically; I imagined it was a huge jungle cat crouched, waiting for me to fall asleep so it could pounce and tear me apart.

My life loosely represented reality and I was going down, quickly. There were no redeeming qualities. I had neither motivation nor direction. It was the agony of defeat. I couldn't bear to continue so I decided that suicide was the only option. I didn't want a messy, violent ending and I didn't know how to get a cyanide pill. My choice was either an overdose from heroin (something I knew absolutely nothing about) or alcohol poisoning. Choosing the latter, I cashed my pay cheque and took every cent to the liquor store.

I purchased a couple of bottles each of tequila, rum and scotch, some cognac, several flats of beer and a bottle of champagne. I proceeded to chug-a-lug myself into oblivion. Somewhere in the process I telephoned several people across Canada. I also telephoned a member of the golf course and asked him to meet me at the clubhouse where there was a board meeting taking place. I had visions of taking some chain from the back of his welding truck and proceeding, Rambo style, into the clubhouse swinging the chain and doing some serious damage. I was homicidal.

26

Something made me think of my father who, after World War II, had made a career out of police work. I ran out the door to the RCMP station that was only a block from my apartment, screaming something like "I do not want to predecease my father."

The police threw me into an isolation cell where I detoxed for several hours. As I lay on the cold cement floor, I distinctly heard the squeaking shoes of the hulking, unsmiling bull-like guard who monitored me. His piercing eyes were like a painting that bores into you no matter where you go in the room. I heard clearly the voices of the officers who transported me to the doctor, "he's pretty big and looks powerful. If he flips we go for his arms."

The officer who sat with me in the waiting room was a member at the golf course. He asked me if I recognized him. I couldn't place him. All I could do was watch my trial on the waiting room television. On my imagined TV show, robed elders examined my life and then pronounced their verdict just before I was admitted to the doctor's office. Their conclusion was that, apart from some minor problems with ethics and morality, it would be okay for me to continue on earth.

The doctor asked if there was a history of insanity in my family. He then suggested that if I wanted to continue to work at the golf course I should shut up, go to the hospital for observation and then return to work in a few days. He definitely needed work on his bedside manner. I must have mumbled something that sounded like agreement because the next thing I knew I was in the hospital. I was assigned to a section that was occupied by elderly patients who were no longer rational so they needed full-time attention. After a couple of days the nurses caught on that I was spitting out their medication. They reported me to the doctor and I was sent home.

My greens chairman said that because my work was excellent, they were prepared to overlook this episode if I returned to work. I had hired a friend from school to serve as my assistant and he had done a good job of filling in for me; however, I was still despondent. I started to drink again and the suicidal thinking returned.

I phoned one of the superintendents who had sponsored me into the Canadian Association. He suggested that I get in a cab and go to a hospital in Edmonton. The sequence here becomes fuzzy.

I was in an extremely crowded psychiatric ward. Then nurses were worrying about me burning myself. I had asked to take a hot shower in an attempt to sober up and clear my head. The next thing I knew I was back in a taxi riding to a detox center. There I sat for hours in a cold, drab waiting room that felt like eternal purgatory. Periodically someone would enter and ask questions of me. It was obvious that I wasn't giving them what they wanted to hear. I finally babbled something about my body being my temple and I wanted to clean it out. Although this kind of talk was foreign to me (I prided myself on having no religious affiliations) whatever I said worked. I found myself in a delousing shower. After my belongings were checked-in, I was issued pajamas and other ill-fitting clothes to wear.

I remember little of my stay there. However, there are vivid memories of the horror stories from my first AA meeting in the detox center. There was also an interview with a counselor who showed me a flip chart image of someone going down the drain of life with an expression of horror as he sank into a swamp of question marks.

I rolled cigarettes with the others and made friends with a woman who had her own problems. After a few days we were taken on an escorted group outing. While outside the center, my new lady friend and I stayed back from the group. We sat and talked and watched the river. We made plans to get together after we were released from treatment. When we returned to detox, well after the group, we discovered we had been kicked out. I would have no shot at treatment this time.

I made my way back home and resumed my pattern. Within days I wrote an extremely profane resignation letter to the board telling them where they could shove their job. When a golf course assistant's position opened up back in Calgary, I accepted it. It was with a superintendent I had known for years. In fact, we had caddied together as teenagers at the Banff Springs Hotel Golf Course. This job didn't work out either.

I resumed my old living arrangements, becoming one of the four roommates in Mo Jangle's house. I was bumped to the smallest bedroom but my old routine was reestablished. Within months I hurt my back, a compensating injury for my misaligned pelvis. It was the second time my back had gone out and it was two months until I could return to work. My winter dragged out.

I had no respect for the mechanic at the course and I had increased responsibilities in equipment maintenance. Grinding reels was not for me. My evenings and weekends were much the same as before and as spring gave way to summer I found myself unhappily supervising a crew that I didn't know. I basically drove around all day in my golf cart and did very little. I couldn't stand it any longer and resigned, leaving my old friend high and dry.

Now in desperation at age thirty-six, I called my parents and asked if I could come home once again, that I wasn't doing well. They consented. This was the end of June. My parents were retired and, in the summers, they spent six to eight weeks living in their mobile home at a fishing camp on Vancouver Island. It was agreed that I could housesit for them until they returned at the end of the season.

The first thing I did was to visit friends in Vancouver. They both worked at the same golf course. One was the superintendent, the other his assistant. I went to their house and drank some beer and smoked some pot. They wanted to go to a neighborhood pub and I reluctantly tagged along. Seated next to us was an ex-NHL goalie that I had met years before at a raft race in Radium. I became paranoid and couldn't muster the guts to talk with him. In fact, I had difficulty being with my old acquaintances. I left the bar, smoked my last half joint and drove to my parent's house vowing never to smoke pot again.

Depression set in and the suicidal thinking returned. I had slowed down to maintenance levels and was drinking less than a case a day. When my parents returned home I lasted another month nursing six-packs of beer in their basement rec room. My obsession with ending my life consumed four or five hours each day. I planned to carbon monoxide myself in mid October when my parents were to be away overnight in Vancouver attending a retired police association function. My mother intuited my intention and persuaded me to see her family doctor. I reluctantly agreed and several days before my intended suicide I opened up to the family doctor. As it turned out, he was on the board of directors of the local treatment center and made arrangements for me to enter that facility the next day, bypassing the regular route via detox.

I had to return to my parent's house for one last night before treatment. I couldn't tell my mother that I was an alcoholic or an addict. I hadn't even acknowledged that to myself yet. I said that the doctor wanted me to attend a substance abuse program because I was having problems like quitting smoking.

This must have been difficult for my parents. Fraser House, the treatment facility, was the former nurses residence annex to the old hospital. It could be seen one block down the hill from my parent's front window. My father's dad, the family hero, had been a surgeon in that same hospital. Having been turned into a community center, the old hospital housed the arts club, of which my mother was president. She was also an active volunteer in the Red Cross. The annex was no longer the nurse's residence; it was Mission's residential treatment center. Now I was a client. I witnessed a new shroud of shame settle on my parents' shoulders. The elephant in the living room trumpeted an end to their comfortable, middle-class existence.

There were three floors to Fraser House: bedrooms, offices, meeting rooms, a kitchen and a dining room. It was a large older house, but for me it was a maze. I kept getting lost the first couple of days. The doctor had placed me on a high level of anti-depressants and I had to be guided around.

It was mid October when I went to my first AA meeting with the guys from the house. I can't remember if it was that night or the next that I stood up, introduced myself and declared for the first time that I was an alcoholic. I was fifty pounds overweight and everything was different. I isolated myself and spent my time reading.

One of the counselors suggested that as well as attending 90 meetings in 90 days I read the first three chapters of the "Twelve by Twelve" every day for 90 days. It was the thinner of the two principle books of Alcoholics Anonymous and contained a chapter on each of the twelve steps and the twelve traditions. (The other AA book was the Big Book that explained how AA worked. It included the stories of the founders and of many other alcoholics).

I agreed to give this a try. I also began to read The Big Book. My day was taking structure. In the morning I had chores and Big Book study, a break and then some lectures. After lunch I had group, then I went swimming and began doing laps. I soon was up to swimming a mile a day. Evenings, we went out in the van and attended AA meetings. My days were full.

My family doctor told me to think of him as a coach. My dentist, thanks to government sponsorship, repaired seventeen years of neglect. My psychiatrist, from the eastern states, believed in prescribing medication. She monitored my progress on a weekly basis. All this looked good, but it began to break down.

The first red flag was alienation from the treatment house group. The director made it known that I was paying for the cost of treatment from my unemployment benefits. He used me as a role model of sorts. This pissed off the other guys who were all on welfare. That instantly made me an outsider.

The second problem was all this God stuff and higher power and admitting our wrongs and making amends to the people we had harmed. That was not for me! If there were a God, there wouldn't be abuse, despair or violence in the world. Kids (like me) would have been safe and happy. It was way too much to comprehend. I didn't think that I could fit the twelve steps into my daily routine. My guard was up and I switched into resistance mode.

I started to see the politics of the house and to openly defy the status quo. Knowing it would piss everyone off, I started to get up early and take a long hot shower every morning. This took all the hot water. At the evening meetings I met people from the larger treatment centre across the river in Abbotsford. Because they criticized Fraser House, I took on their attitudes and started faultfinding, complaining and insisting that the standards be raised.

Eventually I was advised that I might be happier at the other treatment center. That was when something big happened for me. The last line of the paragraph on step one spoke to me. It shouted. Paraphrased it reads something like, "and developed the willingness to listen that only the dying possess."

I was beginning to get familiar with some of the theory and the Jellnick curve on the aspect of "Progression of the Disease of Alcoholism." That frightened me. I could tolerate dying. What I could not tolerate was my imminent future - down and out on skid row in the city, sitting in soiled underwear with my teeth kicked out because I had spoken my mind – okay, mouthed off. We used to call it speaking when we should have been listening. It hit me hard. If this treatment didn't take for me, that was it. I finally realized that I was dying. If I didn't let go of something, death would come sooner than I had thought. The twelve promises made me think that maybe I could have recovery, too.

At the same time that all this was going on, I decided to quit smoking. Several of the residents had tried and given up so there were literally boxes of Nicorettes around. I set a start time of December 3rd and smoked my last cigarette. By Christmas I had quit.

I chewed Nicorettes in a big wad. Heedless of directions, I did it my way. I developed a cheek like a big league pitcher. There were times that I had seven to ten pieces of gum in my mouth at once. In summary, this meant I had eliminated drugs in June, alcohol in October and nicotine in December.

Over those Christmas holidays I received an unexpected gift. My feelings no longer suppressed, the rage and anger emerged. I couldn't take it. Even the anti-depressants were powerless to suppress my volatility. In January of 1986, after three months in treatment, I was admitted to the psychiatric ward in Abbotsford. This was to be my home for the following three months.

I learned the language and moved into a world of "meds" and "sharpies," occupational therapy and group therapy. My psychiatrist tried several types of anti-depressants in hopes of finding the right solution. She bragged about the hospital's psych program but I saw nothing happening. I didn't trust her or any of the psych nurses or therapists and fought them with my silence. The one thing I did respect was the head nurse's refusal to label anyone.

That I was now a permanent resident of the psych ward was another big blow for my parents. After a couple of confrontations, I refused to let them be admitted for visitation. Slowly I improved and was allowed to go out for the occasional AA meeting. By March, I was ready to be released. I made plans to attend the day program at King Haven Treatment Center.

I found a small basement suite and moved in. King Haven wouldn't allow me to live there full-time while I was on medication. In Canada treatment centers aren't affiliated with hospitals. Residents, depending upon policy, can stay for varying lengths of one month, three months or up to one year. This particular center was large with about fifty residents. Their program consisted of chores, a morning AA meeting, afternoon educational seminars and evening AA meetings outside the center.

I was permitted to attend the day program, which meant restricted access to counselors. My outside status gave me a greater sense of freedom and responsibility. My arrival caused no ripples and I slowly became a regular fixture at the center. I attended the meetings, the lectures and even joined some of the small groups and Big Book discussions that were organized. I became known as part of a group that was making good progress due to consistent effort. I was now on welfare and spent the next year committed to this phase of my recovery. I was adapting and meeting new people.

I met a friend in Don R. who had been a heroin junkie for forty years in Vancouver. He was tall, graying and dapper. When he wore his three piece suit he looked like a CEO of a major corporation. He didn't know what a CEO was but was happy when I explained it to him. I gave him rides to meetings and we played a lot of cribbage. He was charismatic and popular so people who associated me with him became more accepting of me. The first time he invited me into his immaculate apartment to play cards he proudly showed me his neatly stocked pantry. At one point before he entered recovery, Don had stepped in front of a speeding city bus in Vancouver. He had done it on purpose saying, "Oh, what the hell." Unfortunately, he later got hooked on painkillers due to chronic back pain from that incident. That was what killed him. He was the first person who really accepted me.

About this time I also took a liking to Cowboy Don who looked like a tall old piece of sinew. He could read and preach the Big Book like no one else I'd met. He'd cackle and point his finger to pertinent paragraphs. Although he was a resident, he was the leader of the centre. He promised if we worked the steps that the compulsion to drink would be like Brussels sprouts. "What do you mean?" we'd ask. He'd reply with a wink of his eye, inquiring how many times a day or a week that we'd even thought about Brussels sprouts. He insisted that the need to drink would be removed and we believed him.

I didn't play cards or really get involved in a lot of the politics at the center. That helped, too. After one of the other day program regulars made me a gift of his Eine Kleine Nacht music, I began to listen to Mozart. Things were going well. I was reading the Big Book once a week and I was opening up to the process of the steps.

When I had been there for a couple of months, my counselor pointed out that my recovery wouldn't actually begin until I became drug free and got off the antidepressants. I duly reported this to my family doctor and psychiatrist. They were enraged. Threatening phone calls and allegations of professional misconduct were traded and I was left perplexed. Then the doctor accused me of manipulation. The treatment centre maintained its position.

To tell the truth I didn't really like being on medication. The side effects were awful. I had dry mouth, knots in my stomach (the effects reminded me of acid that had too much strychnine in it) and I was chronically constipated. I had to fight even to urinate. Because my reaction time was delayed by one or two seconds, I had driven through several lights and stop signs. I was frustrated. I didn't know what to believe. I didn't like being accused of manipulation. All I knew was that I wanted to get better. I was ready to go to any lengths to achieve health. If there was the slightest chance that the medication was hindering my progress, I wanted off.

I no longer trusted my family doctor and I wanted a second opinion. I made an appointment to see the doctor from the treatment centre. At my scheduled time I was left alone in the examination room for a long wait because they had fitted in extra patients. Noticing his copy of medical pharmacopoeia lying on the desk, I looked up the drug that I was currently being prescribed. To my horror, the book said that at the level I was being prescribed I should have been in bed, under the supervision of a nurse. I was at the maximum dosage.

Totally pissed off, I drove to my family doctor's office and demanded to speak with him. (The psychiatrist was unavailable). In a heated conversation, I demanded that he help me wean off the drug. He refused. He advised me that the rebound effect was about 90 percent chance that I'd commit suicide if I went off the drug cold turkey. I asked to be readmitted to the psych ward and be weaned off the drug under supervision. He refused. I became more animated and vociferous. Probably concerned about the patients in his waiting room hearing the commotion, he relented and said he would sign a form for me. Then he sealed the form in an envelope telling me to take it to admitting at Vancouver General Hospital.

I took the papers, drove one block and was broadsided by another car as I went through a red light. The reaction time from the anti-depressants again! I raged at the attending police officer and almost got myself arrested.

My parents consented to drive me into the city the next day and agreed to wait during my interview in admitting. The psychiatrist asked me if I knew what was in the envelope. I told her my intention to get weaned off anti-depressants and all I wanted was the opportunity to try recovery drug free. She listened to what I had to say and then revealed, "These are not general admitting forms. These are committal forms. It requires the signature of two doctors to activate it. In other words, if I sign these papers, you will be committed indefinitely and will only be released when we say you can go."

I couldn't believe it. The betrayal of my family doctor floored me. When I got over the initial shock, the psychiatrist heard my story and listened to what I wanted. She then helped me to devise a plan to wean myself off the drugs and told me what I would most likely go through. She suggested I have a phone in case I needed it and advised me to make constant entries in a journal. She said it would take about a week to get through the worst part. She also indicated that she would phone the family doctor.

My parents had waited the several hours for me and I went home with them. To my surprise I received a phone call from the family doctor. He was full of apology and I could hear fear in his voice. I then received a call from the psychiatrist asking me if the doctor had phoned. She had threatened to report him to the college of physicians and surgeons for overstepping boundaries in areas he had no qualifications to diagnose.

The following day the family doctor phoned and negated his apology of the previous day. All I could do was let it go. The week during which I cold turkeyed from anti-depressants is not in my memory. I don't know if I ate or how I slept. All I remember is blackness, rage and swirling images and sounds. About day three or four, one of the people I usually transported to meetings called and I think I cursed at her. Then, a couple of days later, it was over. I slowly emerged from the cocoon and the world was different.

I've heard it said that the whole reason for treatment is to help the client break denial and accept a higher power so that the process of recovery and transformation can begin. I had finally admitted my powerlessness over drugs and alcohol. Now I truly believed that it took the help of a higher power because it was obvious that no person or drug could fix me, and I had made the decision to allow that higher power to help me.

The members of AA say this much more simply and powerfully, "I came, came to, and came to believe." The first three steps had just worked me. I was now ready to commit to the program and to a new chapter in my recovery journey.

Chapter Two

Level One Recovery

Here I am back at my table looking at the lake. Although there are traces of snow on the sundeck and down on the wharf, the first snow has melted and a second storm is also a memory. The logging clear cuts on the nearby mountain resemble ski runs and I find the illusion comforting, memories of my skiing years bring lots of warm images to mind.

It's nice to entertain some good thoughts because writing chapter one brought up intense feelings for me. The first storm symbolized a time in my life which can still be quite devastating; helplessness, hopelessness and the desire to die in order to stop the pain of a futile existence. A sense of shame pervades and a part of me still aches at the mistake I felt myself to be, even after all these years.

The second storm was more about the present and how I deal with the everyday things that get to me when I am in a vulnerable state such as now. It's early December and I have just phoned my father who lives on the mainland, a six hour journey away. The next day is my birthday and I've phoned to confirm that Kelly and I will be arriving at his house to celebrate an early Christmas.

When we arrived my father made no mention of my birthday. He had forgotten. Hurt, I didn't mention it and I found myself shutting down emotionally. It was becoming another trip from hell. I was entering my sickness and wasn't able to stop it. At some point after dinner he was showing Kelly something and quite loudly added that it was broken–more than likely by me at some point in my childhood. I felt shamed and receded deeper into my bottomless pit of pain. Then, to top it off he gave us our Christmas presents. Kelly received my late mother's cultured pearls; I received a photograph of my mother and myself. Again, in my weakness I saw myself being treated as less than and I was barely able to give my father a hug as we left.

The combination of writing chapter one and the devastation of revisiting my childhood feelings put me in a tailspin.

Back home I was licking my wounds, feelings of rejection, abandonment, and low self-esteem issued forward. I couldn't write and the sense of worthless that I experienced plummeted me into a deep depression.

To make matters even worse I discovered some old letters from 1949 tucked behind the studio photograph. It seemed that my mother had footnoted almost everything in the house for the past several years; we were continually finding her notes of explanation attached to things.

The letters appeared to be warm supportive letters from my grandfather to my father and a part of me pined because I had never had that kind of affection or attention from my dad.

Somewhere along the line I intuited that I needed to write about this setback in order to break through my depression and once again return to the writing of this book. I also needed to move on so that I could build my emotional strength to the point where I could handle the emotional intensity of the Christmas season – I never knew what curves would be thrown at me.

Decorating the cabin for Christmas helped. My mother had been the one who made Christmas at our home and it reconnected me to that old seasonal goodwill. I have to acknowledge that the busyness of decorating helped me make a sizeable shift to my head and helped take me out of my deep feelings. It was all part of self care.

I had been taught at one point that a person's level of recovery (or mental health) is a reflection of the ability to respond rather than react in a given situation. Responding indicates a process of rational thought and appropriate choice. The more work a person has done on his/her life issues, the less likely the trigger is to have emotional impact.

Needless to say the level of a person's vulnerability or emotional detachment is the key factor here. I note this because the first six months in recovery I had come off chemicals as I stopped using street drugs,

38

alcohol, nicotine and caffeine. So when I weaned myself off the medication (anti-depressants), I was for the first time in my adult life, chemical free. I had complete access to my feelings and it was the rude awakening to the beginning of "stage–one" recovery.

I don't know whether I ever felt safe at King Haven. There was a broad cross-section of people there at any given time: street people, convicted felons, pimps, drug dealers, tough guys and suspect business people. Nonetheless, I approached each day there with a consistent effort to participate and learn.

Coming off anti-depressants was the beginning of a new level of recovery for me. The first thing that I had to do was readjust to the intense mood swings that I experienced. There were many times that I had to go home, take a calming shower, climb into bed and listen to the healing sounds of Mozart.

One day after I had been at King Haven for about three months, one of the people that I knew from my Big Book study group approached me on a break. He was a former drug dealer who had taken a big fall. He had lived outdoors in an alley for a year and a half. I wasn't prepared for what he shared with me. He confided that, after extensive observation and familiarization with my story, he knew he hadn't hit as low a bottom as I had. He left me standing open-mouthed.

Shortly after that I had another rude awakening. Father M., an oblate priest, was a guest speaker for one of our afternoon sessions. The Father had extensive experience working with alcoholics and had listened to several thousand recite their fifth step, the exact nature of their wrongs. This particular day he divided the black board in half, one side for happy thoughts, the other side for negative. He listed all the things that the audience called out for each half of the board. At the break, noticing that I hadn't moved, he inquired how I was doing. Near tears, I told him that I identified almost exclusively with the negative side. He said that he understood. He then told me, in no uncertain terms, that I was spiritually bankrupt and that for all intents and purposes I was dead. Here I was, nine months into recovery and a priest was pronouncing me dead. Step one echoed in my ears and I remembered that I needed to develop the ability to listen that only the dying possessed.

These unrelated events prepared me to pay more attention. The words and actions of one of the more flamboyant recovering alcoholics started to filter through to me. He had been a politician. When his life circumstances led him to attempt suicide he woke up in the hospital having had his stomach pumped, gasping, "You had no right." This former leader carried a powerful message. He stressed a few simple directives in recovery: attend meetings, work the steps and do service work. He then insisted that the process of depuking would eventually restore people to something resembling humanness.

This was my signal to enter a new phase of recovery. Eric S. enlisted me as assistant ashtray cleaner at our local home group. After several weeks he suggested that I could help out by transporting a couple of teens to the meetings, make the coffee, set up the chairs and put out the literature. There were dividends to this service work. It reduced my tendency to isolate, gave me a sense of belonging and provided me with purpose.

I was introduced to the concept of three meetings in one. The first meeting is the ten or twenty minutes before the actual meeting begins. You use the time to introduce yourself to someone and say hello. The second is the regular meeting and requires appropriate participation. The third meeting is the time after the meeting. This is when you help clean up, talk to some more people and possibly join a group who are going out for coffee. The three meetings are about involvement, commitment and connection.

I was then asked to do service work at another level. I became the alternate group service representative and I also consented to assist three other people who were carrying the message of recovery within the federal prison on the outskirts of town. In this capacity I became a regular member of the Friday Night Patio Group in Matsqui Prison and began to learn about the fourth step.

Our foursome attending the prison was a good mix. We had an old timer with twenty-five years of sobriety, an established program person with a dozen years, myself and another newcomer. The other newcomer and I shared a common background in sports. He had played some hockey and had also done a lot of skiing – a B Team member in Canada's National Ski program. We had mutual acquaintances and were comfortable with each other.

The old timer was a real Big Book thumper and, despite his evangelistic approach, showed me that someone could stay sober if they followed the program. The other stalwart of our little group took a quiet, yet powerful approach to his recovery. One of the cautions he warned of was ritualizing, like the Pharisees in Egypt, who performed dozens of symbolic offerings each day.

I'm not sure who got the greatest benefit from our service work in the prison. My hunch is that Charley and I received as much as we gave, maybe more. I realized that my anger and bitterness were no different from that evidenced by the inmates. In fact, except for circumstance, it was a classic example of "there, but for the grace of God, go I." I began to realize how judgmental, self-righteous and arrogant I had been.

I received that same piece in another way. I transported several people to meetings as part of my twelfth step work. One of these was an attractive young native woman and mother of three. We had met in aftercare on our release from the hospital. I was attracted to her and spent as much time with her and her kids as I could. It was the closest that I had ever been to being in a relationship, even though it was platonic.

She had been supporting herself and her habit by working the street for years. She spoke the direct, cutting truth that helped her survive that existence. One day she told me, outright, that I was indeed an arrogant, self-righteous so and so, and that I had a long way to go.

Realizations kept coming my way but I felt no closer to understanding the fourth step. My first year cake was approaching and I was getting frustrated. I couldn't understand the process as explained in the literature and I wasn't able to find anyone who could explain it to me. It seemed so overwhelming. I had approached several old timers to act as sponsors yet no one seemed to be able to help me understand the personal inventory and how to go about organizing it.

Throughout my entire journey, whenever I have reached a point where nothing seems to be working and I've been completely frustrated and in utter confusion, something completely unexpected has happened. Then I have received some form of new direction to move to awareness. I now think of these events as spiritual experiences being revealed in their time.

This was such a time. I had spent weeks talking to a minister who I had recruited as a spiritual advisor. I had dumped a lot of anger of the "if there was a God then the world would be a better place, free of violence, abuse, disease" variety. I needed something more.

I had long sensed that native people had a closer relationship with spiritual matters, so I attended a native AA round-up. While there, I inadvertently ended up in the wrong room and was about to leave when I heard the person begin to share. I stood frozen in place, covered in goose bumps, knowing that I had just made a significant discovery. This turned out to be a meeting of Adult Children of Alcoholics (ACOA).

I had related to Alateen speakers before, but the level of sharing I was hearing at ACOA was more intense than the most powerful talks that I was used to. Not one of these speakers was giving a polished performance of "look at how well I've learned to talk." They were risking, expressing feelings, describing their experiences and being real. I listened and cried and, like the people who shared, I felt that I belonged. There was a sense of nurturing, softness and safety - a complete polarity from the angry, aggressive energy I had felt at AA and Narcotics Anonymous meetings. I wanted more.

People at the treatment center didn't want to hear about ACOA. They dumped on it and advised me that AA was the only program. They didn't care if ACOA was a twelve-step program; they had no time for it.

So here I was, in turmoil once again, and it was time for my first year celebration. My mother attended with one of her friends. My dad took a miss. I don't know what I shared from the podium that evening. All I could focus on was the fear in my mother's face and the non-stop wringing of her hands. She gave me a nice card and shared cake with me. She had been supplementing my welfare and had helped me upgrade my car after my accident. She supported me.

My questionable level of sanity was revealed by my car situation. I had always managed to have a vehicle whether it was a three hundred dollar beater or newer vehicle. Once, after being broadsided, my car was still drivable. So I went ahead and drove into Vancouver with my lady friend. While we were getting gas, I was asked to jump-start another vehicle. The cables weren't attached properly and my generator got toasted. I simply took the plates off the dead Oldsmobile and we bussed home.

My mother offered to help me out. I chose another monster car – a Town and Country station wagon that would enable me to transport even more people to meetings. I purchased this lemon through an unscrupulous member of AA, never thinking that a fellow member of a spiritual group would sell me something defective. The transmission on the Town and Country turned out to be in its final miles. Next I upgraded to a new four-door sedan. That car served me well but I couldn't afford the gas it burned so I traded down to a small, poorly maintained sub-compact. I owned four cars in as many months. My mother supported me through this whole process of poor decisions. Her continuing assistance defined unconditional love for me.

This notion of unconditional love was not something I could extend to my AA associates. I began to fault find and see the discrepancies. I began to look at the quantities of coffee and cigarettes these people were consuming. I noticed how they smoked joints and popped pills at the AA dances. I saw how some of the group preyed on women. I saw the limitations that my sponsors displayed through their attacks of rage and impatience. I became disillusioned. They didn't have what I wanted. All I could see was anger and more addictions.

The process of disenchantment was directly proportional to several new things in my focus. The first was the ACOA meetings that I was attending two or three times a week. As a result, I was meeting new people and being exposed to new ideas.

Owen, one of the people I had met through AA, had opened The Serenity Shop, a recovery bookstore. I began to spend time there reading the wide range of books in the store. There was so much information that resonated deeply within me. I had heard seasoned AA members talk about turning to metaphysical interests after they had spent a number of years in recovery and I knew that I wasn't ready for that. However, I still wished to learn more about spirituality.

Owen was a recovering alcoholic with about a dozen years in the program. His business partner, Wanda, was a member of Alanon and her husband was also a recovering alcoholic. They seemed to be on a different level than the people I had been listening to for the past year. I was consistently drawn into the city to learn more.

The storeowners attended spiritual meetings called A Course In Miracles on Monday mornings, alternating their attendance so that one of them was always at the store. I began to attend these meetings too. There I met people who weren't in twelve step programs. They accepted me. After a year in my protected recovery environment it felt good to be around people who lived normal lives. It was doubly encouraging to be allowed into their homes and to be invited back.

Owen had a cabin in the woods near Chilliwack Lake. There was no running water and no electricity. There were two small cabins on the property. He decided to hold retreats for people in ACOA recovery. John Bradshaw had recently been to Victoria, BC. His tapes and video caused lots of excitement.

Owen invited ten men and ten women for a weekend session in the woods. It was a marathon meeting from Friday to Sunday. The men shared one cabin, the women the other. We hauled all our water, chopped wood and cooked on camp stoves. There was an outdoor area with benches and a fire and, weather permitting, we huddled together and talked about our childhoods. In extreme conditions we moved inside. The total cost per person was thirteen dollars for the entire weekend.

The first time I was invited, I was so excited that I could hardly contain myself. This was a pioneering adventure and I was part of it. Friday evening was the introduction that flowed into one long meeting where everyone shared. That first night ran until about one in the morning.

Saturday after a group breakfast, the morning meeting lasted until lunch. Another group effort to assemble lunch, then a second meeting until supper. This was followed by another late night session. Sunday morning was breakfast and a closing meeting followed by lunch and cleanup.

Meeting topics were spontaneous, not planned. For example someone might have been in the outhouse and felt vulnerable because the door never really latched properly. The person might share those feelings of vulnerability and that would become the theme for that session.

There was a beginning, middle and an end. There were lots of hugs and hug breaks and we even had time for singing. We were in the coastal rain forest and there was never any interruption to our weekends. We had the area to ourselves and, as a consequence, people felt safe. There was a sense of belonging.

There became a core group that attended each month and there were always six or eight new faces. We began to have topics for the weekends and even tackled tough issues such as physical and sexual abuse. Each weekend group bonded and Sundays were tearful partings. Sunday evenings and Mondays were vulnerable times back in town - periods of readjustment.

Because I was changing too much to continue the day program at the treatment center, I needed more help - professional help. I decided to move into the city. I advertised for shared accommodation and found an ideal situation in North Vancouver, one block from the bookstore and two blocks from the Alano Recovery Club. I was still attending AA and I asked one of the Course in Miracles students, who was a long-time member of AA, to be my sponsor. She agreed.

Things were moving in my favor. I was getting more support than I had ever felt before in my life. My mother had been like the rock of Gibraltar. Even my father got on the bandwagon. He decided to buy a new car and offered me his Ford Tempo. It was only a few years old and was in immaculate shape. Everything was moving and everything was positive.

My time in the Fraser Valley was drawing to an end and it was more and more apparent that my journey was leading me onward. The local resources were limited and the attraction of larger meetings, different groups, workshops, bookstores, therapy groups and counseling promised new levels of healing. There was a lot of energy moving around and I wanted to be in it and a part of it.

On April 1, a full year after beginning my second time in treatment, I moved my belongings (two suitcases) into Vancouver and prepared for the next step in my recovery journey.

I had been traveling into the city for months, attending both AA and ACOA meetings. I knew the location of the main meetings and felt comfortable branching out. I continued to receive negative feedback from AA members and, as a result, began attending more ACOA groups. My sharing had changed and instead of attempting to parrot recovery talk I began to relate the facts of my childhood.

My service work had suddenly come to an end and I decided to attend a special interest group that focused on the Twelve Concepts of Alcoholics Anonymous. The twelve steps are a group of spiritual guidelines that are known as the program of AA – how it works. The twelve traditions are another set of principles that define conduct – why the program works. The twelve concepts are guidelines for service work and they explain appropriate procedure and levels of authority.

Simultaneously I began to perform service work for ACOA. I became my group representative to the Vancouver area inter-group and attended a monthly business meeting in the city. I also volunteered to do public service speaking to people or agencies requesting information.

This began a busy period of my recovery. In retrospect I understand that the need to do things – to be busy – is proportionate to the level of anxiety. It is a distraction. I was about to become a human doing instead of becoming the human being I so aspired to. I wasn't ready to feel the feelings as much as I had thought I was. I was also dealing vicariously with all the feelings witnessed at the meetings and retreats. Staying busy kept me safe. It kept me out of my feelings.

There was still the constant conflict I was creating at all my AA meetings including my new service meeting. There was a lot of anger – most of it mine. I was advised that if I wanted recovery I had better stick to AA and keep it pure – no outside groups. The Big Book said to avoid anger; it was the dubious luxury of those who could afford it. AA members cautioned against expressing feelings. Don't get too emotional; it's the quick route to relapse. I was also getting static for my increasing involvement in the bookstore. I was reading a lot of books, spending time in the store and continuing to attend meetings and events with the owners.

One day at the bookstore, one of the owners commented that I seemed ready to graduate from AA. I was shocked. Even for me, the idea of leaving AA was a form of heresy. I had bought into the belief that the 12 steps of AA were the only guarantee to remaining sober. Yet, I was intrigued by the alternate choices I was seeing. I wanted more out of life than what I had witnessed in the smoke filled meeting rooms.

I began an active search for professional help. I was living on welfare and resources were limited. I soon learned that the best source of information was the people at meetings and recovery events. The government sponsored help at the Provincial Drug and Alcohol (D and A) Center. Psychiatrists there were free under the government medical plan.

I applied to the D and A program and was placed on their waiting list. Having made appointments to see several psychiatrists, again I had to wait. It is difficult to wait and wait and wait. I wanted help. I wanted health and I wanted to begin life again.

I had been dealing with panic disorder by myself, beginning the process before I moved into the city. The disorder manifested when I was hungry, tired and frustrated. It happened in shopping malls. First, all the sounds in the mall would blend together and I would have to stop moving. Then isolated voices would appear louder than the dull roar. Next I would hallucinate and faces would begin to distort. I would have to find a wall with my back and edge my way outside, where the symptoms would diminish. I would be left feeling scared and anxious.

I slowly got a handle on this by challenging myself to go to malls more frequently and focusing on making a specific purchase. I would talk to as many clerks as possible and, in time, the symptoms abated.

To my surprise none of the psychiatrists were interested in working with me. Each time I waited for the initial interview and each time I was rejected. I was told that they weren't interested in treating alcoholics. They only worked on specific short-term issues; mine were too great and undefined. Try someone else. Eventually I gave up on psychiatrists.

The next resource I tried was a counselor at a provincially funded drug and alcohol centre. There was a three-month limit on their services. They offered one-on-one counseling and some group work. There I asked to see a counselor with a strong background in AA, preferably one who was in recovery herself. Big mistake! I got a middle-aged yuppie with a master's degree. She dressed like a man, wore designer clothes and drove a BMW. Anger and contempt dripped from her demeanor and we clashed almost immediately. She refused to do any anger work with me and I never felt safe sharing anything with her. To make matters worse, she intimidated me. I wasn't sure what to share and my first session was a disaster. I was nervous and confused. I didn't know where to begin.

One of the things that scared me was my lack of knowledge about recovery. I had some basis from the lectures I had received in treatment. I knew that there was a horrible cycle through alcoholism that followed a sequential path known as the Jellinyck curve. It traced the alcoholic's downward progression until it ended in death. One of my major issues was my sexuality — my history of pornography and promiscuous behavior. In my attempt to be vulnerable, I shared this information with her and asked if there was a parallel curve around sexual addiction. Was my fate to become a pervert, a lecher, an exhibitionist or child molester? Was this a predictable path like the spiral for alcoholics? This was big stuff to share.

On my return the next week, the counselor notified me that she felt obligated to report me as a potential sexual deviant. Wow! Where did that come from? My first attempt at therapy and I got dumped on! I felt betrayed and was unable to be open with her again. I had been cautioned against sharing prior to feeling safe. I saw the difference between someone in the care-giving field who worked for money and someone with an interest in providing genuine concern for the client.

The group work was handled by two other counselors and was excellent. I learned some skills and did some good preliminary work. It became apparent that professional help was what I needed and I began searching for appropriate therapists.

A further opportunity was offered through one of the city's universities. The Day House program was intense – six weeks of full day sessions. I was invited to audit one day, and then meet with a psychiatrist for an interview. The interview didn't go well. I was rejected on the basis of my possible volatility. The doctor was concerned that I, or one of his clients, might be injured if I erupted in a rage. His program drew deep feelings from the participants and was sometimes in-your-face conflict. He said he would reconsider me after I worked on my basic core issues.

My rage was pushing up and I felt extremely flushed. I managed to keep it under control and told him that I didn't understand what he meant by issues. Somehow that word seemed foreign to me.

He took the time to describe neglect, abandonment, rejection and several more apparent issues. He said my work was just beginning. His program was designed for people who were seeking closure to prolonged therapy.

He must have seen the hopelessness and disappointment distorting my face. He then did something very kind. He suggested that I search for a counselor or therapist who had worked through his own issues. He warned against getting involved with therapists that only had book knowledge. He confirmed that a good counselor could walk me along the path and advise me each step of the way.

I thanked him and went home to reflect on his words. One of the books I had read said it was important to interview potential therapists to determine if it was possible to develop a therapeutic relationship. It said to ask lots of questions and to state your own needs. I was still smarting from my unsuccessful attempt with the counselor at D and A and resolved to find help, especially with my anger.

My anger was at such a level that I was assessed to be unemployable, possibly for life. As a consequence, I received an extra benefit on my monthly welfare cheque.

Another book I read talked about a leading therapist in the United States who refused to initiate work with any client until they had reached a minimum of one year's sobriety from drugs and alcohol. I had been free of medication for over a year, caffeine and nicotine for eighteen months, two years for street drugs and was fast approaching my two-year cake for alcohol. Deep inside I knew that it was only a matter of time before some new alternative opened up for me. I was ripe and ready to begin. When the student is ready, the teacher appears.

I began attending a drop-in group with a polarity therapist who also led inner child workshops and meditations. She charged a fee for those who could afford it and also offered work to those who were financially challenged. She accepted donations based upon what the client intuitively felt to be right.

I had met her at one of our monthly retreats. At some point, due to criticism by local therapists, we had decided to make the retreats safer by having a professional attend. They donated their services as a means of advertising their skills and attracting new clients, a mutually beneficial arrangement.

After several weeks of the inner child workshop I was invited to begin polarity therapy at a special reduced rate. The purpose of this therapy was to help get me out of my head and into my body.

Then, within weeks, I was also invited to interview at the local Christian Counseling Centre for a partially subsidized opportunity to work with one of the leading counselors in the city. This person was a graduate of Sharon Wegsheider-Cruz's program and offered both one-on-one and workshop opportunities.

My level two recovery was about to begin.

Chapter Three

Level Two Recovery

I'*m enjoying writing these chapter beginnings while seated at my golden pine table looking out the window at the lake. A third storm came through this week to signal the approach of the new chapter. The post-storm melt has already begun. The lake is gray and glassy, the swirling mist lifting, leaving patches of ripples to take charge. The sky reveals oases of blue, hints that a rare, warm and sunny Pacific Northwest coastal day is unfolding.*

Five days from now is Christmas. We have planned something different this year. Last year we opened presents and had our holiday dinner on Christmas Eve. This year we aren't doing presents except for gifts for two of our nieces. We are surprised by the reduced stress we feel from this one decision. Instead of the last-minute bustle and confusion, we have no sense of pressure. We're going to a family dinner tomorrow night that will just about satisfy our seasonal family obligations. Everyone seems happy to be freed this Christmas. We plan a quiet dinner with Kelly's mom, Ann, on Christmas day.

Yesterday, I had breakfast with Kelly and Ann before they drove to Victoria for the day. The occasion was Ann's birthday. They went for a celebratory lunch and a scavenger hunt at a couple of secondhand stores. In keeping with our intention to celebrate simple abundance, we gave Ann the bulk of my mother's costume jewelry. This turned out to be a delightful present; it stirred up nostalgia and provided Ann with several special mementos.

While Kelly was away, I finished the rough draft of chapter two. When she returned home happy and exhausted last night, we talked for a while before bedtime. Both of us are feeling so different right now. The inner calm that we are experiencing is new and beautiful – the tranquility and peacefulness that both of us have always searched for. It has turned out that all we had to do to achieve this was to make a decision, own our power, risk, and begin to do what we wanted to do with our lives, rather than what we thought we were supposed to do. We have no idea where this intention will lead us but we are enjoying this piece of the journey.

I told Kelly that I've been having problems with the writing. In my attempt to let the words flow from my heart, I have worried about my head getting in the way and controlling the process. Consequently, I'm worried about readability and also concerned that, like an inexperienced painter, I'm trapping myself in the corners. It's a lot of extra work to rewrite my way out. Kelly asked if I was connecting with my higher power when I sat down to begin my work. Of course, I had to admit that I keep forgetting to do that.

Today I reminded myself to connect with source. When we moved our table to the lake we brought only four chairs. This morning I am seated at my usual spot in the north. I have asked my higher power to occupy the space to my left. You, the reader, are opposite me in the south. The feminine spot in the west, at my right, is reserved for all the helpful people who are nurturing and supporting me in this effort. I visualize us joining hands. We ask for connection, clarity and direction. I complete my connection by repeating the Serenity Prayer and affirmations.

"God grant me the serenity to accept the things I can not change, courage to change the things I can and the wisdom to know the difference."

"Thy will, not mine, be done."

And, please help me write a significant book with a powerful message that will reach a wide cross-section of people. Please have the right people come forward to edit, publish and market the end result – and please have Oprah's people select it for her book club.

Two other rituals I have incorporated along with a morning yang tea (to heal my sluggish kidneys and increase my energy) are two readings. Each morning I read from Melody Beattie's daily meditation book The Language of Letting Go and follow that with a prayer to join with my guides. Then I choose an angel card to set my daily focus and intention.

Before proceeding further, I want to clarify my intention in writing about Alcoholics Anonymous and its members. AA saved my life, graced me with a spiritual awakening and provided me with a recovery program that I will follow for the balance of my life. I respect and highly regard all those involved in the AA program.

The challenge in writing this book is to clearly present what I experienced, as I experienced it. Each chapter has a slightly different level of consciousness to reflect my progress along the path of recovery and healing. When I speak of moving on from AA and entering level two of my recovery, I need to reveal more information.

I was disillusioned by the drug use I witnessed in AA: the copious amounts of caffeine and nicotine, the sugar, the selective use of pills and pot and the lack of accountability around it all. I became furious when I was told that alcohol was our only focus and that it was not my job to be taking other people's inventories. Well, that just didn't work for me – then or now!

I was also frustrated with my inability to put together a good step four and five. I made several attempts but each came up short and left me feeling incomplete.

At this time I had been attending ACOA, another spiritual program that adapted the same twelve steps as the AA program. In ACOA, people risked sharing their feelings and commented that the truth will set you free. I read new literature and attended workshops that discussed trauma and the silent code of abused children: don't talk, don't trust and don't feel. These professionals were articulating the need to reverse this code. This was the basis of the therapeutic process.

I experienced energy shifts between different twelve step groups. Some groups seemed safer, softer, more nurturing. When I compared this to AA, all I could see from the newcomer to the old timer was anger. That was the prevailing mood just below the veneer of recovery. The Big Book warns of the "dubious luxury of anger." Well-intentioned AA members warned about the intensity of feelings. Expressing feelings was considered to be a quick route to relapse and even death.

Something I heard in a tape by Bob Earl of Los Angeles led me to question the fourth and fifth step process. Everyone I talked to had either a priest or a respected old timer with whom to share that fifth step – the exact nature of their wrongs. In almost every case they talked exclusively about their adolescent and adult transgressions. They gave no voice to their early childhood experiences.

John Bradshaw talked about the sixty thousand hours of childhood and the trauma children experience including physical, sexual, mental and emotional abuse. He suggested the long-term effects were identical to the post-traumatic stress disorder that soldiers and trauma victims experience.

Most children learn not to talk; they internalize their feelings and shut down, leading lives of quiet desperation. The reason that people in recovery were struggling was that they had unresolved issues from childhood. The AA program would not acknowledge it. No feelings were allowed there! The people who were hearing the fifth steps had not worked through their own childhood issues. How could they be expected to help others move through? A teacher can only lead people through to their level of competence. It is then that the student must move on to the next teacher.

It then followed that level one recovery had to do with detoxifying and becoming substance free, including nicotine, caffeine and sugar. Addictions block feelings. This was essential for the true feelings to emerge, the mood swings to stabilize and the stinking thinking to clear. Finally the person would have access to memory. During the year of this process, it is vital to garner as much support as possible to begin the spiritual program of recovery as offered by Alcoholics Anonymous.

The first three steps of AA are designed to do the same thing that treatment centers are expected to accomplish – they break an individual's denial and show him that there are no quick fixes. There are no pills, people or external sources to magically eliminate the condition; however there is help available. The help can only come from a higher power that dwells within each person.

It is essential for the person to come to believe in a higher power, to form a relationship with that power, ask for help and trust the process.

Level two was the next phase – doing the work – in ACOA. That was the feeling work around the family of origin issues. I continued to follow the twelve steps, to recollect the experiences of childhood and to release all the emotional baggage that was negatively impacting my present and future.

Sharon Wegsheider-Cruz (whose husband, Joseph, was founder of the Betty Ford Clinic) once stated, "Recovery isn't for wimps." It takes courage and support from both sponsors and professional counselors to do the work. The pain of transformation can be beyond description. Someone told me that we only go through as much as we can bear at any given time. This pain and fear leads to the exact nature of our wrongs. Until the pain is released it continues to control us, immobilize and even kill us. It is the source of our rage and acting out. It defines how we function as adults. It robs us of our joy and happiness and prevents us from self-actualization. We manifest this pain as disease and addictions.

With the same fervor that I made the effort to get off my medication and attempt drug-free recovery, I jumped into my new phase of recovery. I received a sign that was significant for me. I now view it as a signal from my higher power to pursue this turn in the path.

The apartment I lived in had a playground adjacent to my window. One morning I watched two toddlers playing with their trucks in the sand box. All of a sudden the older one reached over and slapped the younger one across the side of the head. The younger one cried for about two or three minutes and then picked his truck back up and the two resumed their play. It was so simple yet so profound. A boundary had been crossed, a consequence had taken place and some feelings had been expressed, then it was over. Nothing had been internalized. It showed me the simplicity of the process.

I was apprehensive and confused about joining ACOA. Neither of my parents was alcoholic, yet I related to all of the characteristics that were described in the ACOA books. Moreover, I was even more frozen, shutdown and damaged than most of the people I met at meetings. Thanks to my program of self-education I began to understand why this was so. I was reading voraciously and always had one or two of the ACOA primer books on the go. I also joined a series of orientation workshops that served as a focal point for learning the issues and doing the work.

Apart from learning the basic premise "don't talk, don't trust and don't feel" I began to look at family life. Where was I in the birth order?

This was said to indicate my role in the family. The first-born is the hero, the second the cute one or mascot, then the scapegoat, then the lost child. I learned that, as an only child in a dysfunctional family, I qualified as a survivor doing double duty. I played all the roles.

Another concept that determined my path came from my reading and education process. I learned to develop a holistic approach to recovery. Simply put, I needed to focus on various levels of recovery: physical, mental, emotional and spiritual.

Let me remind you, I was on welfare and had the time and desire to go to any lengths to achieve health. Mere abstention was not enough for me.

I was concerned with my physical health. I needed to lose weight, increase my level of exercise and repair the multiple levels of physical damage done by my addiction cycle. A good weight for me ranges from one hundred and ninety to two hundred pounds. I have a large frame and because I played sports I have an athletic build. When I first entered recovery I weighed two hundred and forty pounds. In the treatment house, before I entered the psych ward, I had begun swimming. That was relatively inexpensive exercise and I was comfortable with it. As a teenager I had been a lifeguard so I was accustomed to swimming lengths. In my twenties I had been active in seasonal sports and was familiar with the concept of a repetitive daily routine.

Things seemed more expensive in the city and I wanted some variety in my exercise regimen. The logical solution both for my limited budget and my need for routine was walking. There is a phenomenal seawall around Stanley Park, a historical land grant that borders Vancouver's downtown core. Approximately fourteen kilometers in length, it took me about two to two and a half hours each day to walk the wall. I slotted my walk in for late mornings. This became the core of my timetable and I managed everything else around it. For the next three years, this was my daily exercise program. Regardless of rain, snow, wind, sun, I loved the sea air, the seagulls, the trees and the cliffs. My weight gradually came off and I stabilized at one hundred and ninety pounds.

Another significant part of my physical wellness program had to do with repairing past damage. Initially in treatment I had my teeth repaired – that was the visible part. The new focus, based on my reading, had to do with rebalancing the neurotransmitters in my brain. There are dozens of neurotransmitters, but some are more essential to happiness and well being than others.

My research indicated that drug use, especially cocaine, depleted these transmitters. The body does not replenish them; when they are gone, that's it. Fortunately there was a medical doctor who had a process of measuring which neurotransmitters were absent. Working in conjunction with naturopaths, he had a plan for reintroducing and stabilizing the neurotransmitter levels.

The machine his assistant used was called a Vega tester. It looked like a fountain pen with a cord attached to a simple view meter (a needle on a scale). He found that my levels were significantly low for six major neurotransmitters. I entered his program and had two neurotransmitters rebalanced simultaneously every six months for the next year and a half. All I needed to do was take some drops daily and follow a special diet.

The diet was designed in conjunction with a test for allergies. I tested allergic to wheat (glutens) and dairy. During this course of treatment, my diet consisted of rice and vegetables with small amounts of meat. No sugar, no coffee. I purchased several stacking bamboo steamers and found the diet easy to incorporate into my lifestyle. Each morning, I simply chopped some veggies, put them in the steamer and put rice on to cook. By the time I got out of the shower, breakfast was ready. Even the clean up time was minimal. Perfect for me. This diet was also a big part of why I shed the pounds so quickly.

Several of the neurotransmitters that I received therapy for were seratonin, gabba norepinephrine and dopamine. Another element that was revealed in this process was my high level of candida albicans – a yeast disease. It can cause confused thinking, irritability and depression. Through this period, I also began treatment for candida and balanced my diet with a non-dairy yogurt fortified with acidophilus.

The light switch recovery response to this regime did not materialize. But my general health, sense of well-being and happiness, slowly made a marked shift. Like everything else, it was not in my time, but in the natural progression of events – in nature's time.

The mental approach was a continuation of my educational process. I read as much spiritual and recovery literature as possible. I had access to a wide variety due to my friendship with the owners of a spiritual bookstore. I accumulated a recovery library that included dozens of cassette tapes and some videos.

I became a workshop junkie, attending meetings, seminars and any program that I could worm my way into. I was consistently warned that all this head stuff would more than likely have the reverse effect. This caution came both from program people and professionals who warned me about analysis paralysis. A few suggested that I was lost in my head and that head recovery was antithetical to feeling work. They were right. But, like the song says, "I had to do it my way." I rejected the counsel of others and chalked it up to unsolicited advice.

My study of A Course in Miracles (ACIM) continued for about a year. I attempted to trudge through the workbook. I wrote each day's lesson in the margin around the page. What that means is, I wrote the entire content of each page in the skimpy margin at the top, bottom and sides of each page, in miniature writing. I considered this to be an active meditation and was my daily ritual after breakfast. It took one or two hours of my morning. I also read complementary literature relating to the Course. I worked at the journey without distance, referring to the concept that most people are emotionally unavailable even to themselves. The distance is the journey from head to heart, an essential trip if one is to attempt the feeling work.

I also incorporated into my study a poster by Louise Hay called Loving Treatment and read it every morning while I toweled off after my shower. Hay's message is "if we are willing to do the mental work, almost anything can be healed." Her best seller *You Can Heal Your Life* and *Heal Your Body* were essential additions to my library. She, along with Bernie Segal, were doing what no one else could – getting people who were suffering from AIDS into permanent remission. I loved Hay's concept of cleaning house. She stated that it didn't matter what room of our house we began in, if we got the necessary tools and began the work, that eventually the whole house would become clean.

I also decided to do some recreational reading and got hold of the complete works of Charles Dickens – all seventeen books – and proceeded to devour them.

The emotional component was my weakest area. I had read that denial can be a blessing – there are so many levels to it. It is suggested that each survivor is a genius and his unconscious knows the exact protection to keep him safe. My entire life I had been taunted with being too sensitive. Alternatively, I had been told in recovery that my childlike honesty would be one of the keys to a successful recovery. I had a hard time reconciling this, as I didn't consider myself particularly honest. As a drunk I had been quite a bull shitter. I'd lie, cheat and steal any time I got cornered – anything to avoid accountability.

I now avoided that which I wanted most – access to my feelings. Once in awhile something would trigger my emotions and I would emit deep, visceral emotions – the gut wrenching variety that would double me up and simultaneously produce about five pounds of snot a minute.

Once at a weekend workshop, we spent Friday evening hearing about anger and what it felt like as it surged through the body. When Saturday morning came, a trigger was hit. I virtually erupted. The facilitating counselors assessed me as ripe to do the work. They appointed me to be first to swing the tennis racket at a pile of sofa cushions. The intensity was profound. This level of emoting became my goal. I had secretly envied the people who had easy access to this level of feeling. It seemed to me that they were winning the game of recovery. I wasn't getting it that my busyness and consistent chaos were distractions that were holding me back. I eventually learned that this too would pass.

The other aspect of my emotional work was with professionals. I was attending an inner child workshop one evening per week and receiving a session of polarity body work every other week. They were both designed to help me make the shift from head to heart, to being in my body. The therapist knew I was sabotaging this part of my recovery. If I wasn't intellectualizing and rationalizing and justifying my experience, I was then either lost in the past or flying ahead to the future. Before I could move through this part of the journey, I had to learn to exist in the present and get out of my head.

Another level of therapy with Paul Kaufman at Burnaby Christian Counseling was two-dimensional. I joined a group called Breaking Free of Codependency for a three-month session. This was based on the work of Sharon Cruz. In this format, each member of the group became a star for one session; later they supported all the other members when it was their turn to do the work. Apart from the Breaking Free group, I did one-on-one counseling that was a combination of education, processing daily events and attempting to do the feeling work of childhood.

My primary therapist had a rule that I couldn't see other therapists while I was doing this process. However, I got his consent to do the polarity work at the same time. Now this may seem like a lot all at once. It was, but I wanted even more.

When another therapist, John Arnold, offered to help out, I got consent to bring him on board as well and arranged for him to attend our retreats. He was a recent transplant from Los Angeles who wanted to get his family away from the rising level of violence there.

Arnold was different from the others. He practiced Yogic Reichian Therapy. Wilhelm Reich had been a rebel student of Freud's. He had bounced around Europe before ending up in America. Basically Reich believed that people held fear in their bodies in certain identifiable patterns and that through touch and a safe environment the fear could be released. Eventually his eccentric ideas of recovery got him in trouble with the law. Reich died in prison.

Now I had added another session of bodywork to my week that included another evening session of group work. My week was more than complete – it was bulging. I had everything timed and managed. The plus side of being a control addict is excessive organization. If you think that I had too much going on, there's more to come.

Before I begin to talk about the spiritual level of my holistic approach, I need to clarify that I got all this help organized while I was on welfare. My therapists all gave me sliding scale deals and offered much of the work for free. There were costs that were beyond my means and, once again, my parents supported me. It probably cost them several hundred dollars a month for about two years. We initially attempted to keep track of the cost, and it was my intention to repay them, but it got lost along the way. I think my mother was happy to know that I was getting the help I needed.

I had so much going on that it felt like I was in graduate school. The opportunity to do this level of healing was incredible. It was the most significant challenge of my life.The final aspect of my holistic approach was the spiritual level. This formerly bankrupt part of my program was taking shape. As I made the shift from AA to ACOA, I also began to attend Codependent's Anonymous (CoDA), another spiritually based twelve-step group for people who were having problems in developing relationships. Now in my late thirties, apart from attempting to make a career out of being one of the boys and committing full time to drugs and alcohol, I had never had a genuine relationship with a woman.

Except for my mother, until the age of eighteen I really didn't know a lot about members of the opposite sex. I was so busy trying to be accepted by my male peers that apart from one-night stands and the occasional short term coupling, I was literally alone out in left field.

It became obvious to me that my unresolved childhood issues had ill prepared me for adulthood. As a matter of fact, it was embarrassing to realize that I had to complete the balance of my teenage maturation process in my thirties. Drugs and alcohol had stopped this process. Now that I was clean and sober, I had to complete the stages. Yes, I had problems developing and maintaining relationships as an adult. I now recognize this as level three recovery. I wanted to attract a partner into my life so I decided to include codependency work in my curriculum.

Just when you think I've had enough, there's more. A new workbook came out from people in California and it was hot. Called *Twelve Steps – The Way Out*, it was exactly what I had been waiting for – a workbook that helped people through a series of questions on each of the steps of recovery. There was a commitment period of six to twelve months and the participants formed small family groups meeting weekly to advance the process. I saw huge excitement and energy around two books in my years with the bookstore. This was one. The other was John Bradshaw's *The Family*. Of course I had to find a group and begin this work.

By this time I had let go of my Course In Miracles group, but I did continue that workbook on my own for some time.

The final piece I attempted to work into my ever-expanding portfolio of recovery was an attempt at a relationship. I began to include Jackie, a young French Canadian woman who was a recent immigrant from Los Angeles, in my daily walk around the sea wall. She was in the group therapy session with me, belonged to the same writing workshop that I did, and attended my ACOA meeting. She and her sister Jillian were completely enmeshed. The sister resented my involvement and association. She too, was in the group, the workbook and the meeting.

Things were about to get very interesting. I attended retreats once a month, worked part time for the bookstore and tried to squeeze in every recovery opportunity and workshop that came my way. I was committing to service work and also attempting to develop friendships along the way.

I had more than a little on my plate. I was completely overextended. I loved it. My life was full and I was fast tracking my way to recovery.

I entered recovery in October 1985 and moved into Vancouver by April of 1987. I had most of these recovery modalities in place by the end of that year. This neatly maintained the chaos called my wellness program until January of 1990.

I thrived on the busyness and for the first time in my life I felt in charge of my own destiny. This was different from the alternate lifestyle I attempted during the late sixties and the "can't remember seventies." The crazy thing is, this period was when I was supposed to be letting go and letting God.

The one thing that I do know is that this time was, in spite the pain of remembering childhood trauma, probably the happiest time of my life as it was unfolding. There is nothing in my drug and alcohol era that even remotely compares. Like many other people in recovery at that time, I felt like a pioneer. I personally met John Bradshaw, Terry Kellogg, John Lee and Jane Middleton-Moz. I read their books, did their workshops and I discovered incredible things about myself.

I initially had difficulty coming to terms with a concept expressed by Kellogg in a video with John Bradshaw. He said that there is one relationship that we can develop that will never leave us. That relationship was the one we have with ourselves. Every other relationship will either die or fade with time.

That idea led us at the retreats to begin a process of self-nurturing. As Gay Hendricks said in his book we had to learn to love ourselves. We even chose a theme song "The Greatest Gift of All" and then there was the hug song. We were all getting carried away and even bought teddy bears. I had a closet full of old golf sweaters that I still wore. I purchased butterfly appliqués and had them sewn over the course insignias and logos.

One book I never read but loved the title became a new philosophy for me. The book was Dr. Jess Lair's *What You Think Of Me Is None Of My Business."*

I was high on life and high on recovery. There were a lot of ups and downs. I was certainly riding the pink cloud that I had been warned about in AA. I didn't care. My life was changing and I knew that it was mega times better than the insanity, depression and suicidal thinking I had survived two years earlier.

I'm not sure if I felt as good as Joe Namath but in my own way I couldn't wait until tomorrow. I was getting better looking everyday. This is big stuff coming from the guy who, if he saw himself in the mirror while going to the bathroom at the disco, had to go home because he couldn't stand what he saw. I knew that no one would want to dance with me. Now I was the butterfly in metamorphosis. It was my turn.

Chapter Four

Beginning The Work

There is a luminescence behind the slumbering mountains that speaks a simple truth; somewhere the rising sun is already washing morning shadows away. The lake lies quiet, a flat gray mirror supporting smoky swirls of mist that coyly allow glimpses of its deepest secrets.

There is no storm to usher in this chapter; no melt to wash it clean. Instead, the mist catches the first rays of sun as they flood over the ridge. The wispy veil is transformed into a thick, cloud-like canopy that conceals the surface of the lake.

The whole picture spills through the front window of the cabin and washes over me as I sit, pencil in hand, at my pine table. This dynamic metaphor is a portrait of my denial system. Like the mist, denial can shift from transparency through translucency, from opaqueness and back again, resting when the need for emotional stability dictates.

My knowingness that protected my inner child knew when to permit fragments of trauma to bob to the surface and to control how big they became. The process was unpredictable and not on a nine-to-five schedule. Stuff came up when it was ready. It was nicer to have this happen in the safety and privacy of counseling sessions or when sharing in workshop groups or talking with friends. It was inconvenient and frightening when it happened in the middle of the night. In public, like while waiting in line at the bank or at the supermarket, it was downright intrusive.

Once the process begins it can't be reversed. It takes on a life of its own and may be managed, but never controlled. Once the denial had lifted it might return intermittently to cloud issues and provide temporary solace. However, there was no going back to blissful ignorance. Slowly, piece-by-piece, the release and healing would take place.

I was awkward in adjusting to this process. Part of me was embarrassed that I had to go through this. I was ashamed that I wasn't as healthy as everyone else in the world appeared to be. I wasn't comfortable in the starting gate. I wanted to be farther down the road, or better still, approaching the finish line.

The concept of journey rather than destination began to have meaning for me. The realization that the journey would last as long as I live took the pressure off me. Without the struggle to arrive at a destination, the journey could be pleasurable.

Prior to grasping this concept, I had tried to force the issues to surface, to perform for the therapists, to please the people in my therapy groups. I wanted to emote at will and make the all-star recovery team so I could jump to the big time and become a touring lecturer and recovery guru. That is not the road to recovery – at least it wasn't my road.

We get to choose what we want to be or do in life. My recovery process formed around this universal law, designed by me, for me, by my inner genius without any interference from my rational, intellectual thinking self. Each of us is exactly where we are supposed to be. Things are revealed in their appropriate time.

Getting back to 1987, I had settled into my apartment and found evening twelve-step meetings that felt right for me. My basic expenses were covered. My part time work at the bookstore related to my recovery process and paid me cash. I had integrated the walking program, healthy eating and spiritual reading into my daily wellness plan. Education and therapy were my next challenges to overcome.

Because of my sensitivity, I searched for knowledgeable counselors who were prominent in the city and who had worked on their own issues. The styles and techniques of my three therapists touched different parts of me and provided a well-rounded approach. The therapists knew each other, shared a common respect and consented to work with me simultaneously. This placed me in a high-energy curve where I thrived.

In that year and a half while I received polarity therapy, I made a slow transition from my head to my heart. When I first began, I used the words *thinking* and *feeling* as though they were interchangeable. For example, I might say, "I feel you should do this."

Earlier in the educational process at the Drug and Alcohol center, we were given handouts with little cartoon faces to illustrate feelings: happy, sad, angry, fearful, and so on. Somehow it hadn't filtered through to me that thinking is for thoughts and feeling is for emotions.

Patricia, my Polarity therapist, gently challenged me by asking in which part of the body I located each feeling. Slowly I was able to make a shift, like dropping a bad habit. Similarly she taught me breathing to focus on different parts of my body where I held tension and stress. While she applied the bodywork; I breathed and a perceptible sense of release would occur. This procedure released daily stress and tension, but more importantly it addressed trauma at a cellular level. Sometimes the work was verbal and detached and at other times it was deep, emotional and visceral. More often than not it was a slow, gradual process of release.

The work was consistent, slow and safe. While I opened up more and more, I formed an intimate, therapeutic relationship with Patricia. She slowly nurtured me to health, allowing me to go at my own pace by providing consistent, gentle support. She listened to what I had to say, validated my experiences and seldom, if ever, judged me. Her stuff didn't get in the way and there was never an indication of power or control. There was cross-over from my other therapies, but it was from this gentle woman that I learned for the first time to be gentle with myself.

This allowed me to soften to the point where I began a process of self-care. I learned to reframe many of my unhealthy beliefs and my anger and control issues diminished. I learned self-care and how to nurture myself. I reprogrammed my inner voices and took responsibility for taking care of myself in new ways.

This process is called reparenting. I allowed myself to accept that I had an inner child and undertook the responsibility to educate and raise that child. I also committed to doing the emotional work.

Much of this was facilitated through Patricia's inner child group meditations. We would begin with a complete body relaxation, working up from our feet to the top of our heads. We would then remember some aspect of our childhood experience. She focused on basic developmental stages. Each week we would connect with a stage, learn the appropriate developmental skills and then give ourselves permission to see how that stage had played out in our actual lives. When the meditation was over we formed a circle and shared our experiences.

There is a powerful healing energy in groups such as this. Each person's story touches places in the heart and vicarious healing is experienced. We learned that we each have male and female aspects. Everything shared is a part of the whole – part of our whole experience.

Like the retreats I had attended, there was a core group of people at these weekly evening meditation sessions. As the weeks became months, we evolved into a family of sorts. On a new level, we began to develop healthy group intimacy with a positive, dynamic experience. We laughed together, cried together, grieved and hoped. It was an exponential foundation for later development of healthy relationships.

The beauty of Patricia's work will remain with me always. Over time I learned that she too had struggled, as do all single parents. Yet, she never allowed that to get in the way. She offered her services on a sliding fee scale and only charged what people could afford – what she called an intuitive donation. This kindness applied equally to her group participants and to her one-on-one clients.

When I knew it was time to enter a new phase and reenter the work world, our time came to a natural conclusion. Each of us knew that it was time for me to move on. Our experience ended as gently as it began. This taught me that I could be open, safely express my feelings in an appropriate setting and allow myself to trust another human being. Her unconditional love and support helped me begin to accept myself.

I had been connected to the Christian Center agency through an ACOA member. My work with Paul Kaufman, the therapist there, was different. We sat in a cold, impersonal cubicle. He took notes while we were videotaped. Each session ran for an hour. That was more of a head experience for me. The therapist attempted to get me to my feelings and occasionally I would succeed. There was also group work.

At any rate, I felt obligated with Paul to emote on demand. The people in his group turned the tears on and off at every session; I don't know whether they were real or phony. Because I was expected to be continually crying and releasing, I underwent an experience of continuous performance anxiety.

Paul did everything he could to make me feel safe. He did all the right things but I couldn't allow myself to be vulnerable. I don't think it was because of him – it had more to do with my life experience around male energy. This had been a constant testing ground and had usually ended in either betrayal or violence.

As a consequence, I remained in my victim role and used the sessions to debrief the chaos and dysfunction in my day-to-day life. He taught me much about the position of victim, the need to triangulate and form alliances to create power and control in relationships. I learned to see the unhealthy dynamics I was acting out on a daily basis.

These sessions were likely as difficult and frustrating for him as they were for me. I expected to do core level feeling work and move quickly through my stuff. He had committed to me to continue the work for as long as I needed the sessions. Our work, however, continued along the lines of educational tutoring, denial breaking and occasionally doing some feeling work. He helped me develop strategies to handle the chaos in my life and taught me the perspective of detached observation. Through this, I learned to own my stuff and describe my feelings in emotional situations without attacking the other person.

Paul used a model called the DESI method, an acronym for: Describe the experience; Express my feelings; Suggest a solution; and Involve the other person. Instead, I used this model to triangulate against him. I talked to a couple of other people who were seeing him. These people were as *stuck* as I was and both had left therapy. I accused the therapist of only being able to take us part way and questioned his competence.

I had been seeing him for over a year and like my other therapists I was paying him on a sliding scale based upon what I could afford. My self-esteem was low and I interpreted this situation as a power position – rather a lack of power position. If I had more money and was paying a higher rate for sessions I'd surely be getting better therapy and doing better in life. This was my rationalization.

I was more successful in his group work where I completed two of his six-month sessions on psychodrama. In the first I set up a scenario and had people role play the important individuals in my life including my inner child. I did the release work by pounding the pillows with a taped-up plastic baseball bat.

The second six-month session of group psychodrama was a different experience. Instead of repeating the anger work, I had no need to swing the bat. Instead the dynamics changed; I cried and cried. The group of twelve lifted me in their arms and gently nurtured me while singing soft lullabies.

Paul was exceptionally skilled at group work. He knew what each person needed to experience in his or her turn at being the star. I witnessed unique experiences for each of the twenty-four people who participated, twelve in each session. Each person was honored in a special way on his day. At the end of each session, recommendations were made to each individual in the group.

I wasn't expecting the feedback I was offered at the end of the second session. He told me, in front of the group, that my time had come to end and that I needed to move on. I almost threw up. I got very cold and lost the ability to hear him talk. I knew he was still going around the circle giving recommendations. Somehow I was able to wait until the last person had been addressed. I knew I had to say something so I stepped into the circle and asked to speak.

I said I was startled by his recommendation. I don't know how clean I was but I continued to speak. I said that it was cruel to terminate me in this manner, that it would have been kinder, softer, more appropriate to tell me in my one-on-one session. I was angry; I don't know if I swore or not. Feelings of rejection, betrayal and abandonment left me cold. That was where it ended. I felt that he broke his commitment to me.

I had to meet him once again in a professional capacity to tape a seminar for him before he left for a new career opportunity in Mississippi. I had told this person my life story. I had been vulnerable in his presence. He had seen me rage and he had seen me grieve. He had taught me so much yet I couldn't allow myself to get close to him. All the boundary work! All the debriefing! All the strategies for coping! It was this therapist that emphasized: the measure of a person's recovery is his ability to respond rather than to react in a given situation.

When I left his therapeutic counsel I was still heavily into the reactive phase. Years later I have a better handle on things and like to think that I respond more than I react. Someday I hope to be able to respond appropriately to this therapist and thank him for the work he did with me.

The third therapist I was privileged to work with was very different.

John Arnold was tall, lean and, although he was Caucasian, he was a practicing Sikh who wore a turban, a beard, had the long hair and braided sideburns tied under his chin. He had investigated a wide range of therapeutic modalities and spiritual practices. He had left Los Angeles to live in Vancouver and he possessed a remarkably eclectic approach to healing.

Essentially he was a yogic, Reichian Therapist. He incorporated much of the work of Alexander Louen, one of Reich's star students. The process he used was to facilitate the release of fear from clients. He believed that fear, when internalized, was stored at a cellular level in holding patterns within the body. The particular holding patterns revealed the nature of the trauma and abuse. Each was related to behavioral characteristics.

John performed his therapy in the basement of his home. Each session began with a verbal update – a holistic barometer of my mood and vulnerability. This was followed by a series of stretches, exercises and breathing to prepare me for the release phase. Then, I would lay on my back with my knees bent, similar to a position of a woman receiving an examination by her gynecologist. He would then adjust my leg position by pushing on the inside of my knees. I would begin to shake.

It was his theory that this shaking was the stored fear releasing from my cellular memory. It related to the term "shaking in their boots" from the movie westerns I watched as a child. The shaking could last from fifteen minutes to over half an hour. John manipulated my knee position and occasionally directed my breathing. Sometimes he asked questions; other times I shared feelings. Sometimes I simply lay there and shook in quiet. Occasionally these sessions were followed by periods of deep, visceral emoting. They were always a complete physical, mental and emotional drain. After each session I went home to bed until the next day.

One evening a week I met with John Arnold's group. These groups had been assembled with people from the retreats I attended and from various recovery groups around the city. Each group was limited to eight people who made a commitment to meet for a minimum of one year. There was no furniture in the room where we convened, only large pillows on the floor.

The only rule was that we could not get up during the sessions or leave our spot. Each group formed its own dynamics with each member taking on his or her roles. These were roles that each of us had learned in our family systems. We had projected our learned roles into all of our circumstances from school to work to relationships.

Not surprisingly, the dynamics of each week's group revolved around our dysfunctional patterns. Anger was the predominant emotion and rage was often the climactic trigger, which released our emotional response. We learned that anger was a secondary emotion and that it always protected us from either fear or pain. Once the fear or pain was allowed out it could be released.

The magic of group dynamics was powerful. Whenever one person had the release, it opened that aspect for other group members to release a similar memory of pain or fear from their past.

There was considerable controversy within the healing community as to whether John's cutting edge work was beneficial or traumatizing. It was too intense for many of the clients and the dropout rate was high. Many clients were advised by their primary therapists to discontinue. There were always people on the wait list to join either of the two groups and invariably the session framework remained constant – only the faces changed.

John offered a gong meditation one Friday, each month. The Tibetan gong he used was huge, four or five feet in diameter. It produced a range of sounds that were as compelling as an orchestra. Again, these sessions were preceded by a series of stretches and exercises to prepare each individual for the release work. Then, everyone lay on the floor with his or her feet toward the gong. The energy and sounds from the gong lasted about an hour. Then everyone shared his or her experience.

There was a broad range of responses to these gong sessions varying from spectacularly creative intellectual insights to powerful emotional releases. Invariably there was a sense of calm and emotional well being. It felt good, like the effects of listening to Mozart or Gregorian chants or the soothing sounds of new age music.

My work with John Arnold was longer term than with my other two counselors and the scope was also broader. At times he served as mentor and cautioned me about becoming involved in practices that seemed to be cult oriented. He helped me prepare life strategies and deal with relationship conflicts. He also advised me that my brutal honesty sometimes hurt people. He suggested for me to ponder the idea that honesty without compassion is cruelty. He offered future goal oriented strategies such as learning the art of superficial conversation.

He accepted the task of helping me to rebuild myself as an adult. This was the next logical step after re-parenting my inner child that I had started earlier in therapy. He told me of the trends in Los Angeles and the work being done by many of the powerful movie industry people. He provided me with exclusive documentary videos that examined the efforts of celebrities who were going through similar change, and he instilled the confidence in me that I was going through parallel transformations.

John also served as a spiritual advisor. His own search had led him through many explorations on his way to embracing the Sikh philosophy. He pushed none of this on me, however, merely allowing me to explore things in my own way and in my own time. He did offer significant insight into basic spiritual laws. The one that jumped out for me was "there is a spiritual law that guarantees that if a person does the best he can in everything that he faces, things will work out in his best interest, for his highest good."

Before I had moved into the city, a native elder who was a member of AA once told me that he saw in me a beautiful stallion who had his will broken by a harsh handler of horses. It follows that the work I was now doing was core stuff around my self-esteem, confidence and building my hope for the future.

Throughout my life I had held on to the saying that good things come to those who wait. I was now beginning to see that I had never really waited for anything. In fact, my life experience had been a continual misadventure based on my self-will running riot.

I can't remember how or when I met John Arnold, but I was one of the first people he met in Vancouver. I had invited him to be part of our group retreats that were organized out of the bookstore. The groups and my one-on-one work had been an offshoot of that introduction. Needless to say, I put extraordinary effort into my work with him. Over the years I saw him, I also forged skills that would later serve me in healthy relationship development.

There were problems that arose and they were beginning to surface not only with John but also with other people that I was attempting to form relationships with.

I saw Owen, the owner of the bookstore, as a father figure. Because of this, my relationship with him was confused. Initially we began developing our friendship as we attended A Course in Miracles meetings.

He had about a dozen years in recovery; I had about two. As our friendship evolved, he asked if I was interested in learning how to operate his audio equipment and helping him tape keynote speakers. The tapes would be sold at literature tables at conventions and roundups that he was invited to. I saw this as a way of broadening my horizons and supplementing my meager income.

We began locally and I enjoyed meeting the organizers, speakers and attendees at the events. At first I could barely talk to people. Then, when I had a table between us and I could talk about external things such as the tapes and books, it became easier. Eventually I was able to talk to people one-on-one. This was huge for me. All my life, especially in my drinking days, I had hidden in groups. I could relate a story in a group and then drop back into obscurity and let someone else take over. Now, I was having actual conversations with people. I had developed a bad habit of talking down to people; now I was learning how to communicate appropriately and actually respond to what they were saying. The communication skills I had been taught as part of my after-care program when released from the psych ward were beginning to pay dividends.

My conversations with Owen, as a consequence, were becoming more real and even I could see the growth. One particular trip comes to mind. We had traveled to a Vancouver Island ACOA event and Owen had forgotten the name of his contact person and where the event was being held. I offered a number of solutions from my perspective but he dismissed them all. When we arrived in the town, he pulled into an ice cream parlor and said he had to go to the bathroom. When he came out of the restroom he walked up to the counter and asked the teenage girl where the ACOA convention was being held.

I wondered, "What is he doing? She's a teenager – this is an ice cream parlor – what would they know about recovery programs – surely there was a Alano Club or somewhere we could get some real advice."

To my astonishment she replied to him, "Oh, it's at the high school, about three blocks from here."

It turned out that the meeting committee had ordered a special ice cream cake for their celebrations. Our higher power had led us to the perfect place to ask advice. It was simple and easy. This lesson was characteristic of the teachings I was receiving.

I soon reached the point where I was traveling around the province handling the events, sometimes alone and sometimes with a helper for the larger ones. I also flew to the Yukon with Owen's partner. Each event taught me lessons and my confidence grew.

The retreats had evolved, as had my level of participation. I was part of the organizational committee and I provided leadership during the weekends. As a result my relationship with Owen became increasingly involved. There were differences of opinion and complications arose. It was only a matter of time before conflict and toxicity became apparent. We had moved from addressing issues to choosing politically correct positions within the group. Resentments were beginning to develop and they were being gunny sacked rather than resolved.

At the same time that tension was building in the bookstore, a couple of other stages were being set up. At the simpler level, I was handling myself and practicing healthy recovery skills. But, the more complicated and emotional my life became, the more it shifted toward drama and chaos.

I previously mentioned the excitement caused by the twelve-step recovery workbook. When it finally arrived at the bookstore, we were all anxious to begin the process. Owen organized the first group in the city consisting of a number of people I knew plus several counselors and therapists. I was not included in the group. I was crushed. My childhood betrayal and rejection issues surfaced and I began to act out negatively toward him. My fault finding, blaming and repressed anger escalated and my relationship with him quickly deteriorated both at the retreats and the bookstore.

I joined the second workbook group, which was organized by Owen's brother and began a systematic process of working through the twelve steps. However, the damage had been done and my relationship issues were spilling out. I became polarized from a counselor who was also participating within the group. I attempted a new strategy for dealing with the conflict.

Instead of responding to the group member directly, I was advised to let him vent at will. We thought that sooner or later he would let out enough rope to hang himself. This was a new strategy for me; I found it equally difficult to neither defend myself nor engage him in conflict. In spite of the difficulty, I persisted in my non-violent stand. Within a matter of weeks, the conflicted group member raged out, never to return. I must have handled it well because I received positive feedback from group members for modeling a healthier approach. In fact, the person's wife was part of my small group. Although we were somewhat distanced, she continued with us until the end of the workbook.

I wasn't as fortunate in my initial attempt at a relationship with a woman. Two sisters, Jackie and Jillian, who had been attending ACOA also joined the step study group. One was in my small family group and the other was part of the group with the person who had been in conflict with me. I was about to learn about enmeshment. Both sisters were passionate and dedicated recovery people. They were emotionally spirited women of Italian-French Canadian descent. They were also quite attractive. I was pleasantly flattered when Jackie, the sister from the other group, began to phone me. We slowly formed a friendship. We occasionally went for coffee after the group ended and spent a lot of time talking on the telephone. We decided to become co-sponsors.

In ACOA, the sponsorship affiliation between members was different from AA, where an experienced group member helped a newcomer along. In AA, there was a spoken policy that it wasn't wise for males and females to enter into this form of sponsorship. In ACOA, which was a new twelve-step group and didn't really have old timers, there needed to be an alternative approach. It was felt by many Codependents Anonymous (CoDA) members that the old way was a set-up for power and control. Hence, the concept of two equally positioned people serving as support to each other became the norm in CoDA.

So, in our co-sponsor relationship, Jackie and I had increasingly expanding contact. We met daily and walked around the seawall bordering Stanley Park. This walk usually took about two and a half hours. In our walks we discussed the questions and answers that were presented in the workbook. We also talked incessantly about our childhood experiences. We didn't always see eye-to-eye and there were some stormy scenes and split ups in the middle of our walks.

I was beginning to learn how to be with a woman on a daily basis starting at the basics. I had no idea of how to connect and no experience of maintaining eye contact. These were as foreign to me as her Italian heritage. She would get furious with me when I was unable to connect meaningfully with her.

At the same time that I was learning this lesson, the Gulf War was underway.

From listening to psychiatrist Sonia Freedman doing counseling by telephone on CNN, I learned that men and women were raised differently. Women look each other in the eye and speak from their hearts. Men look away from each other and speak about things from their heads. In time, I extrapolated this knowledge to understand how to connect to a person. I was in my late thirties.

To complicate the relationship with Jackie further, the two sisters joined the groups that I was attending with John Arnold, my Reichian therapist. Initially we were in the same group but as the dynamics emerged, Jillian switched to another group. She remained in my writing workshop family group, however, and the dynamics and tension carried over.

Jackie, Jillian and I formed the perfect triangle. I wanted an exclusive relationship with my co-sponsor. Unfortunately, as the intimacy between us developed, so did the friction from the other sister. Jillian, of course, wanted an exclusive relationship with her sister and wanted me out of the picture. Jackie was caught in the middle and wanted a relationship with each of us.

This triangle also became apparent at the bookstore. There were Owen, his partner and I. These triangles surfaced at the retreats between Owen and one of the main organizers and me. The universe was giving me an awareness of how denial patterns are revealed, step-by-step. This, of course, implied accountability for setting up and seeing my projections. I had to admit that yes, I was projecting these situations and becoming an active participant. I also had to say, yes, I was an only child and I came from a family system that was a triangle – my father, my mother and me.

This all happened about the same time that I was working through the questions on step four of the workbook. These included investigating my control issues, anger, repressed sexuality, fears and inhibitions. I had also been examining my family of origin and was beginning to understand my own family system. In fact, I had also been studying my mother and father's lives to get a better understanding of the dynamics they each contributed to my family system.

I knew that my childhood issues were impacting my adult relationships. I had no doubt that, unless I began to do more work on this, I would never establish a healthy relationship. For me life was no longer worth living in the isolation of addiction and denial. It was all or nothing. That's another fourth step issue from the workbook – all or none thinking.

I was primed and ready for the conclusion of the fourth step, prepared to do my first significant fifth step. My first had been with a minister who simply listened to my litany of transgressions. This time, my fifth step advisor was to be Father M., a priest with extensive fifth step experience. He was the same priest who had pronounced me spiritually dead at the treatment center a couple of years earlier.

Both the relationship with Owen and his partner, and the relationship with Jackie and her sister were beginning to resemble my relationship with my parents. The key words here would be toxic and distant, if not non-existent.

My other significant relationships weren't going well either. These included the one I had with my higher power – a very flaky relationship that reflected the low level of faith and trust I was able to sustain; and the relationship I had with myself. I had initiated the re-parenting work, undertaken the challenge to learn the basics of communication skills and had begun to glean as much self-esteem and confidence as my journey had permitted me to grasp. It was still a shaky, unstable connection.

I was marginally surviving in a protective recovery bubble. I despised the dog-eat-dog world of normalcy but I renewed my pledge to become healthy.

With several years of abstinence, my body was free of alcohol and drugs, including nicotine and caffeine. The twelve-step program was the cornerstone of my foundation and spirituality was my focus. The fellowship of the program and the contacts from recovery-based activities constituted the core of my social interactions. I pursued educational avenues to widen my understanding of my life and sought the counsel of professional therapists to assist me along my path.

There had been major turning points beginning with the decision to pursue recovery, enter treatment and join AA. There was the controversy about medication and my decision to stand up to the medical profession and follow the advice of the addiction specialists from the treatment center. Then the difficult decision to move on from AA and begin the family of origin work and continue the program through ACOA.

As my denial began to give way to awareness, I saw that the unhealthy survival mechanisms and distorted belief systems formed during childhood were negatively impacting my day-to-day life experiences as an adult. I was unable to develop any sense of healthy relationship. I realized once again that my life was unmanageable and I needed to shift my focus toward the twelve-step program that dealt with these unhealthy behaviors: CoDA.

I had already been attending CoDA meetings and I now knew there were two options available to me – continue to do the work and progress or remain stuck in isolation, loneliness and unhappiness. The choice was obvious. I had seen people unwilling to move beyond AA who remained stuck – addicted to caffeine, nicotine, chaos and denial, their feelings unavailable even to themselves. I saw them as angry abstainers and I refused to limit myself as they had.

So, with renewed commitment to my higher power and trust in the process, I prepared for a new level of consciousness. I was now ready to look deeper and do the Relationship Recovery Work in CoDA. I saw this as Level III Recovery.

PART TWO

LEARNING TO FEEL

Chapter Five

Releasing The Past

It's a good day to be inside. The rain is lashing down sideways, slanting into the choppy lake below. A heavy fog hangs over the opposite shore, hiding the mountains beyond. Just past the slick planks of our deck, the branches of the huge cedar tree dance wildly in time with the frantic melody of our wind chimes. On the lake, a tree trunk races by the cabin propelled by unseen spirits madly paddling ahead of the fury of the storm. The valley is awash with this purge, bringing the promise of renewal.

Like the valley, we are cleansing ourselves as we enter the new year. The seasonal bacchanal of rich foods, sugary desserts and constant snacking have reduced our sense of well being to a memory; bloating and acidity bear witness to our powerlessness over food. Headaches, clouded thinking and lethargy have regained their hold on us. Now the residual effects of our holiday bingeing are flushed from our systems and our blood sugar levels regain a semblance of stability. We feel compassion for those who take the seasonal cultural psychosis to the level of compulsive overspending and alcohol abuse. We vow that we will someday control our emotional medication with food.

While this has been a relatively quiet season for us, at present we have difficulty in not taking on the emotional turmoil of Kelly's extended family. We hooked into toxic family issues between Kelly's dad and brother-in-law and our skills as support people were put to the test. Fortunately we disengaged by drawing the line between care giving and care taking.

Now staying clear of the toxic storm feels like another test. It seems that these issues threaten to do us damage if we fail. Then I remind myself that we are not on earth to pass tests – that old way of thinking produces fear and negativity. Our purpose on earth is to realize that we are spiritual beings with a duty to create. When I regain this perspective, it becomes easier to move into my writing. Fear has a negative quality that jabs deeply into my conscience. I recognize that this fear had been censoring what I revealed about myself and family of origin.

I have a higher power. I have formed a spiritual synergism with a group and I have asked that only those messages that are helpful to the intent of this book be revealed. I now must trust that whatever flows through me will pass my integrity and discernment.

Listening (or reading) is for learning; speaking is for healing. Now is the time for me to proceed with telling my story.

The fifth step process caused considerable activity in the small family groups (four to six people) that were forging through the Twelve Steps – The Way Out workbooks. Our fears were reduced by the act of following the workbook. There were a variety of issues that people discussed within their family group structures. Talking through these issues was like releasing a pressure valve. It transformed the ominous task of revealing secrets into simply being part of the process. The desire to dump old baggage and the promise of a healing tranquility prompted everyone along.

I was no different. I booked an afternoon with Father M. It was gratifying to be sharing my stuff with someone who had been through the fifth step several thousand times with others. I wasn't concerned that he was an oblate priest. I actually felt more connected to him because of a mitigating physical limitation that caused him to be relegated to working with alcoholics. He was another human being who had been poorly treated by an insensitive bureaucratic system.

Over the years, Father M. had built Bountiful House into a healing center in a remodeled building in the heart of the city's east end, an area occupied by transients, derelicts and addicts. His staff of counselors were well qualified and they made an excellent team.

Nevertheless , I was nervous. Father M. worked repeatedly to keep me out of my head. He challenged me every time I used phrases like "I think" or "I believe." Slowly over an afternoon, he dragged the pertinent facts out of my past. The process that he employed included jotting key phrases and words on a blackboard. My openness was directly proportional to the quantity of words on the board. Through my tears, he filled that space with the evidence of the ghosts of my past.

Upon completion he asked me to sit quietly while he reviewed the board. He then said that what he was about to tell me had no basis in judgment – that he would merely be mirroring back what I had disclosed to him. "But before I begin," he said, "I have one question that I'd like you to answer."

"Okay," I replied.

"Where does your mother live?"

I told him that she lived with my father in the Fraser Valley about a one-hour drive from the city.

"Where else does she live?" he inquired, a slight smile on his face.

I was tired and confused. His message was not hitting target. I told him so.

"In your head," he said. "Your mother lives in your head as much as she lives in her home with your father."

The nice thing about priests is that when they shank you in the guts, they don't turn the blade. The effect his words had on me were obvious. I made a mental note to thank my polarity therapist for her work in bringing me to the level of feelings. I was fully present rather than being stuck in my head on this one.

That gut shot left me numb; I tolerated the balance of Father M's feedback from somewhere on the ceiling, knowing full well that I wasn't the detached observer, nor was I rocketed into the fourth dimension as Bill W. described in the Big Book of AA. However, I was undeniably split from my body. To make matters worse, if this kindly priest was right, I had lived the greater portion of my life in an uncharted dimension of my own mind.

Glimpses of reality had previously filtered through the web of my denial over the years and dealt me similar truths; however, I had easily dismissed them. Labels like mama's boy, daydreamer and too sensitive had hit home to some degree. Behind the labels was the darkness of the void.

As a child, there were times that I hated to go to bed at night because when I closed my eyes I seemed to shrink to the size of a grain of sand.

Everything faded to blackness and seemed far away while still being within reach. It felt like I was outside, looking into myself; that blackness was the emptiness inside me. It was a recurring terror. I could never describe it so that my mother could understand what I was experiencing. I felt alone and powerless in that place. I hated to go to bed.

Now, all that I had learned began to filter through. What I had experienced as a child was the hole, the blackness, the void. Nothing could fill that emptiness. Its name was the deprivation of hope, sense of self. There was no way out – no exit. No amount of anything tangible or material could fill that hole, nor could an emotional Band-aid heal the gnawing emptiness. At the core was the hollowness of my addiction. That's where I was empty.

Somewhere in my childhood a sequence of damaging events had occurred. As Dr. Phil eloquently expresses, it only takes a few seconds to get burned and the scars remain for life. These traumatic incidents or repeated sequences of incidents can lead to post traumatic stress disorder.

When co-dependency was first discussed there was confusion over defining the condition. Each author or therapist had a different perspective. Some of the definitions were succinct, others more elaborate.

I found myself in the middle of this cognitive confusion. All I could remember about co-dependency were the buzz phrases: lack of identity, loss of self, emptiness, void, victim leading to rebellion, acting-out, delinquent behavior, set-up for addiction, the abused child becomes an abusing adult, offender status, substance abuser. The words swirled in my head like mosquitoes until I wanted to run away from them, arms flailing, nearly delirious in trying to escape the revelation of my life motivators.

I realized that I had recognizable patterns in my personality and behavior. I was split from my body and reality. My ability to be in the moment was nil.

I wanted to hide my insecurities from the world. During my childhood, my father hadn't earned much money and we existed near the poverty line. As an adult, I took on the personality of my mother, learned to make do, endure and stretch the dollar. I attempted to make things look better than they were. When I wasn't involved in impression management, I compared myself to others and I attempted to social climb my way out of my bleak existence. The dishonesty and futility of my desperation led to an overdeveloped sense of responsibility. Like my mom, I gave a hundred and fifty per cent effort in hopes of achieving a passing level of acceptance.

My anger, frustration, and abusive nature came from my father's side

86

of the scenario. A lifetime of compromising and kowtowing to the military and police systems had left him volatile and abrasive, a cross between Archie Bunker and Ernest Borgnine.

Somewhere in between was the lost child, too hurt and scared to claim his own spot in the sandbox of life. John Bradshaw's lectures on soul murder returned to memory. An infant human would be not raised as carefully as a newly discovered hybrid rose that would be nurtured and supported by loving horticulturists.

I wasn't sure that my parents had wanted me. They were married in May and I was born in December of the same year. Even if my math or dates were wrong, I felt that I wasn't okay. I was likely the product of unprotected sex, a mistake. Probably the reason that my parents married was to cover up their transgression. Who paid the price? I did. If I was the mistake, my birth symbolized passing on the family legacy of shame. Shame is about being a mistake.

One minute there is love, the next there is fear: mixed messages, inconsistencies and betrayals. This precious little hybrid rose was not the recipient of consistent nurturing and support. He was not protected. He was bullied, shamed, brutalized and betrayed. As a result, a beautiful child was slowly poisoned to the beauty of the world and disciplined into delinquency, anger, rage and addictions.

Spirit indeed! My soul had been murdered as my life had been controlled and programmed. I grieved when I saw athletes receiving Olympic gold or actors accepting their Oscars. The child within me experienced the pain of disconnection from self, and the loss of ability to develop talents and self-actualize.

Somehow I got out of Bountiful House that afternoon of the fifth step with Father M. Instead of driving home, I navigated downtown traffic and parked. For two hours I walked the sea wall and took the refreshing sea air deeply into my body. It seemed vital to be outside and in the proximity of other people.

So many thoughts raced through my mind. When is it parenting and when is it abuse? What about all the good times? Why am I so damaged? Why did I persist in suicidal thinking? Will it ever end?

There was so much information that brought up so many more questions. I needed time for the dust to settle. But before I went home, I needed to put the afternoon's process into a new perspective.

The workbook, workshops, retreats, weekend groups, meetings, and all the history discussed in therapy threw more information into the air. Add to that the nightmare of my life and the emptiness of my existence.

In the midst of all this confusion, I had a goose bump belief that what Father M. had told me was the key to my dilemma. It then dawned on me that to understand myself I had to understand my parents. I had to look at them and gain a sense of their origins. Then, hopefully, I could let it all go and begin to reconstruct my own life.

As I began my walk, I reviewed what I had uncovered about my parents.

As a young child, my mother had immigrated to Canada from Sweden. Her father had been a land rich, cash poor farmer who had leased out sections of his property. He and his first wife had several children before she became terminally ill. To care for her and manage his house, he hired a live-in nurse. Upon the death of his first wife, my grandfather married the nurse. She bore him four more children, two boys and two girls. The younger girl became my mother.

The older children from the first wife immigrated to the U.S. where they all gained prominence. Their families became successful: business people, politicians, a commercial artist, an engineer and an airline pilot.

The nurse's children came to Canada with her and their father. These children's attempts at enterprise all floundered. There was a failed sawmill operation and a shoddy cottage industry based on an orchard and a hen house.

It must have been difficult to get my grandfather's affection. All four of these children recreated the nurse situation in their lives as adults. The oldest brother married his neighbor – both she and her sister were nurses. His second daughter and son both became nurses. My mother's older sister became a nurse. My mother, always the impression manager, upped the ante by marrying a doctor's son. Her other suitor was an alcoholic businessman. The youngest brother was a tail gunner who was shot down over Germany and died in World War II.

My paternal grandfather was a sober, hard worker from a family of eleven. He was sponsored through medical school by an anonymous family benefactor. He married and moved to British Columbia, settling first on Vancouver Island, where my father was born, then shortly afterward settled in the Fraser Valley east of Vancouver. Like many relatives on his side of the family, he became a professional person.

As the family hero, he set the bar high. He was a surgeon and physician with a rare talent for percussing, a method of diagnosing patients. He declined a lucrative practice in Vancouver's affluent neighborhood of Shaugnessy and passed on other business opportunities. Instead, he set up a practice in the small suburb of Mission. There he enjoyed small town life and had the leisure to pursue his many outside interests. He was a low handicap golfer, a deacon in the Baptist church, a grand mason and a reserve medical officer in the army. He and my grandmother produced two children: my father, William, the oldest and physically larger child; and Ted (Edward), my namesake.

When World War II began, my father enlisted in the infantry and his brother Ted became a pilot. Before seeing action, Uncle Ted was killed in a training accident while flying over Calgary. Coincidentally, I crashed and hit bottom several decades later at the Calgary golf course.

Although my father rose through the ranks and earned a battlefield commission, this was no solace to my grandfather. He had taken his younger son Ted's death very hard. He became despondent, eventually having a stroke and losing partial use of his right arm. As a result, he was unable to perform as a surgeon and his medical practice declined. Ultimately he was admitted to a sanitarium after being discovered walking around his large home slashing things with a knife. He died in the mid 1950's.

My grandfather was overcommitted to his work and didn't have enough time for all of his pursuits, his practice and his family. Something had to give. My father's need for attention is probably due to neglect suffered in his childhood home. Further to this, I learned from a family friend that my grandfather was a rager; he would often explode if someone misplayed a hand during a game of contract bridge. My father apparently received the brunt of this violence and refused to play social cards as an adult.

My father also survived the war and the death of his brother but not the loss of his father's attention. I believe that these loses were internalized and never adequately grieved. My father had always been jealous of his younger brother who clearly enjoyed the favored relationship with my grandfather. When I was born, I was named after this favorite brother. That made me a target for my father's negative feelings.

In our nuclear family, my father and I competed for my mother's affection; she was forced to divide her time between us. There was constant tension in my childhood home. My father was angry, belligerent and abrasive.

He began a pattern of strappings, intimidation and threats that never let up for my entire childhood. My father used two barbershop straps to discipline me. He would threaten to pull down my pants and spank me in front of company or friends. Not only did these scenes occur in our home, but he also did this with people present outside the house. I later learned in therapy that this is a form of sexual abuse.

My father, always an avid reader, had a large stock of reading material at home including cheap, smutty magazines and soft-core pornography. As a teen I became addicted to these off-color publications.

Parents are supposed to protect children. They are not supposed to hurt them, betray them, abuse them or use them to meet their own needs.

Fortunately my father, like his father, was rarely at home. He did a lot of shift work and, in his time off, usually went hunting or fishing. Life was nicer, meals were better and my home was safer when he wasn't around. When he was home he wasn't really there. He sat in his chair and read or watched television or did both at the same time. I learned to be quiet around him and coexist without being noticed.

When I was born, my father was in the BC Provincial Police and we lived in the northern part of British Columbia. When that police force was disbanded, my father joined the Royal Canadian Mounted Police. Apart from the long hours and rotating shift work, he was required to make court appearances in his time off to testify at trials. The long hours, lack of sleep and stress caught up to my father, eventually causing him to resign from the RCMP.

After a brief stint as a bus driver, my father joined the Royal Canadian Air Force (RCAF) and continued his career as a military police officer. We usually lived for two or three years on any one base, then were transferred.

He enlisted in Vancouver and it was there that I began school. As a rural-based, only child, I had limited social skills. I was afraid of other kids. I wanted to play with them but didn't know how.

When I was 7 years old, my father was transferred to Europe for a year. While he was away, my mother and I lived in a Vancouver basement suite. My mother helped out with the owner's two daughters while the owner worked. Apart from my parents, this was my first social triangle. Joan, the elder daughter hated me because I played with her sister, Judy, who was my age. I felt that something was wrong with me and I learned what it was to be attacked.

After my father returned from Europe, we lived for two years on a base near Montreal. We didn't have enough rank and family size points to qualify for base housing. That meant we had to live off base in an entirely French community. From there, I bussed to school for grades two and three.

My father strapped me if I didn't have a straight A report card. I looked and acted like a bright student; I wore glasses and got the highest marks in the class. My classmates and neighbors picked on me, calling me grandpa. There were two English-speaking boys my own age who were each nice to me if the other wasn't around. I was cast into another triangle where I often played alone or went home crying. It was crazy making. Here, I wasn't okay because I was English-speaking. The French kids pushed me around and I normalized the idea of being bullied.

Our next posting was in New Brunswick where we got a house on base. At first it seemed great. We finally made it into private, married quarters (PMQ). We lived in a section with privates, corporals and their families. The non-commissioned officers and officers lived in nicer homes several blocks from us. This taught me that I wasn't as good as other people. The families close by were like us. Their parents had some high school education or, like my father who was a sergeant, had completed high school. The pay was low and conditions were bleak. There was alcoholism and family violence. The kids acted out their parent's issues. I wound up in the middle of it all.

It's not fun to be the new kid on the block. It's worse when the others discover that you're a cop's kid. I survived grade four but my attitude declined in grade five. Although I still managed to get the highest grades in my class, I participated in anti-social behaviors, theft and violence.

By grade six I couldn't stand the violence around me any longer. I started to drink Drambuie from my dad's liquor stock, mixing that with rye and beer. In an attempt to bond with my oppressors and stop the bullying, I joined a gang. We slicked our hair back in ducktails, smoked, drank and stole money to support our drinking and smoking habits. We bullied weaker kids and began to sexualize with the willing girls. The back of a building or a dark parking lot was an opportunity for a grope or more.

I despised my parents and fantasized about killing them with a shotgun while they were sleeping. I decided that I would no longer try to succeed in school or anywhere else. To hurt my parents, I planned never to accomplish anything in my life. I wanted to rob them of the pleasure they might derive of my getting married or having children.

In grade seven, I got my father in deep trouble with the RCAF. My friend and I barged in on the commanding officer's daughter in her home while she was baby-sitting. Against her protests, we drank all of her parent's liquor and then left her with the mess. The next day, my dad was called to account in front of the commanding officer. Shortly afterward we were transferred to another base, this time in Ontario.

At the Ontario posting we again didn't qualify for base housing and had to live in the small city adjoining the base. We rented the main floor of a house in a working class section of the city. Here I was again the out-of-place new kid on the block. I had a difficult time adjusting. By end of grade eight, I had a new level of respect beaten into me by my peers.

After a year's adjustment to the new environment I was still a punk with my hair slicked back – a Fonzy wanna-be among Richie Cunningham middle class values. One positive here was that I had temporarily stopped drinking.

Attempting to bond with a new set of oppressors – the wise mouthed, cool, cruel athletic crowd – I resolved to take up sports. I had no basics, no fundamentals and my learning was accompanied by a lot of shame and embarrassment. Team sports were humiliating, but I eventually made the teams and began assimilating as much as possible. I also got a part time job in a butcher shop on weekends. This gave me a little spending money – enough to buy some designer clothes like the cool kids wore.

My grades had gotten progressively worse from grade six when I had decided it wasn't cool to be smart. I made it through grade nine and ten without doing my homework. I was constantly acting out in class, trying to get noticed by being funny.

In grade eleven, I began to fail. At the end of that school year we were transferred to a small radar base in a mining community in northern Quebec. There, I was put back a grade in school because of my poor marks. At this Protestant school, there was a dress code; we wore ties and slacks to school. Although I became school president, I had conflicts with all of my teachers and the principal. Just after Christmas I was expelled after I broke another student's nose while playing basketball.

In the new year, I was accepted on probation at the Catholic school in town. There were only four kids in my class. We shared our math time with grade eleven so at times there were up to a dozen in the group. Some of our classes were in English, others in French. We had two sets of notebooks for each subject. In the morning we placed all of our notebooks, open, on a table to show that we had completed our homework. If the homework wasn't done, we couldn't attend school until it was completed. This was my first real structure at school. I initially rebelled at the prayers before and after each class. However my grades began to improve. Finally, I was getting nineties and one hundreds in math.

On a different level, I began playing individual sports. I became a lifeguard and learned to ski. I also worked as a disc jockey for two years at the local volunteer radio station. Everyday after school I hosted a radio show and played the top ten hits. Then I swam lengths for an hour, went home, ate and did my homework. We had no television because my father refused to pay for French reception.

The off side to attending the French Catholic school was that I was English-speaking and a Protestant. The parents of the French Catholic girls wouldn't let me date their daughters and the French guys made a sport of ganging up on the English students.

I started to drink again. We could buy quarts of beer in the grocery store. Sometimes cabaret owners would let us go in to dance.

When I was eighteen, we were transferred to Vancouver Island for my dad's final military posting at Comox. I had a very confusing year and didn't get much schooling in. I got a job at Safeway, bought a car, made several new friends and played sports.

The following year I left for Notre Dame University in eastern British Columbia. There, my drinking led to drug abuse. I dropped out in my fourth year and floundered until I entered recovery. Throughout my early adulthood, I was unwilling to face any of my problems.

Part of my denial came from minimizing and discounting uncomfortable situations. I mastered the art of justifying and rationalizing events, putting the right amount of spin on things to make it seem all right. I could recognize this process beginning in my mind. It was part of my survival technique, my defense mechanism to protect me from further pain.

Years later, Father M's feedback after our fifth step session made sense to me. These weren't only survival skills; they were the nature of my problem. I split from myself and became my mother with her habits of making do, making things okay. I was the master of "grin and bear it."

The insidious nature of the disease is much the same as that described for alcoholics in the Big Book. One minute they are sober and have been for years; the next thing they know they are drinking. They refer to alcohol as cunning, baffling and powerful. I knew full well that I was witnessing a parallel condition with my thinking process. I had slipped into my disease – my co-dependent behavior.

The impression management side that controlled my perceptions clouded my vision. In the cognitive process, I doubted myself and all the therapy work that I had done. The jaws of denial snapped shut as powerfully and as quickly as a swamp gator.

My mother, from a comfortable position behind her wall of denial, insisted that there were no problems in our household while I was growing up. She maintained that my problems began when I left home for university and began drinking.

My memory came to my assistance and reminded me what I had learned from recovery books and listening to the thousands of hours of sharing by people in meetings. It doesn't matter how one person's story differs from another's. There is no degree of abuse; there is no best-worst story. Each person's story is as personally significant as another's is to them. Siblings raised in the same family under the same conditions have different stories, memories and events. In fact, they often seem like they came from different families. This is due to the roles they played in the family system. This holds true for twins who each have their own perspective.

I was emotionally wounded and the impact on me was significant. I also appeared to have undergone a prolonged history of feeling alone, unsupported and violated. I had been repeatedly shamed, humiliated and scorned. To add insult to injury, I had been beaten, intimidated and threatened. My parents had been rigid, controlling and authoritarian. My father's philosophy was "jump when I say jump and ask how high when you're in the air." I had been called "lost cause," "dead loss," "dirty little sod" and I had been spanked, bare butt, in front of guests in our home. The injury and violation covered the full extent of my being – physical, mental, emotional, sexual and spiritual.

The words of Alice Miller, the German psychiatrist, in her book *For Their Own Good* came flooding back to me. What she proved wrong was that children do remember the harsh corporal punishment liberally administered in their youth. She insisted that children remember the rigid, authoritarian family systems that were the set up for dysfunction.

As if I needed more proof, my higher power provided another shred of evidence, in living color. As I completed the end of my seawall walk, I had a chance encounter with a former acquaintance.

Near the last corner on the sea wall I met a person I had known from my partying days in the mid seventies. We called this guy Kamikaze Shirley because of his insistence to take it to the limit. This guy, although in his thirties, could have passed as a double for Willie Nelson, with the fine long hair, wrinkled skin and beard. He was from a rigid, authoritarian German background. He and his brother owned a repair business and Shirley had an apartment above the shop. He boasted the longest continuous party in town. A large portion of his sinus cavity was lost due to his high level use of coke.

He had just been refused entry through international customs and was attempting to figure out how he was going to get on a plane for his vacation down south. We chatted about mutual acquaintances and I told him about the fifth step process I had completed that very afternoon. We went our separate ways into our separate realities.

While I knew that I could never be fixed and that there was no external source that could remove the devastation of my past, I finally believed that life could be improved dramatically. That's the nice thing about hitting bottom – there are only two ways to go – out through suicide or up through recovery.

The revelations of my walk reaffirmed my belief in the process; my faith in my higher power was restored. A calm came over me and I basked in the beauty of nature in the middle of the city. I returned home, exhausted, ready for sleep, calmed by the healing tranquility that had been promised as my reward for completing the step.

Meanwhile, back at the cabin, I look up. Outside my window the sun is shining and the lake is still and calm.

Chapter Six

Level Three Recovery

*I*t's a gray day at the cabin. Although yesterday was beautiful, today the weather has slipped back into characteristic seasonal dullness. A light mist is rising on the lake and a heavier blanket of cloud rests on the trees that solemnly guard the water. The mountains aren't visible and it's difficult to predict whether there will be afternoon sun.

I'm feeling much the same. Yesterday we celebrated the finish of chapter five by taking the afternoon off and going for a long walk along the edge of the lake and into the old-growth forest. We tried to walk home by the highway loop but the traffic ran by us too loud and too fast, threatening our peaceful mood. We retraced our steps around the lake edge and discovered we had to ascend a fairly steep hill. We had been unaware of descending the hill earlier as we had been preoccupied, comparing the lake view to the one we enjoyed at home. The downhill trek had gone by easily and quickly but coming back up was a different story.

Life is like that. We can do a significant piece of work or establish a healthy routine but, unless the effort is sustained, there is a gradual shift back toward the unhealthy behavior. Our daily walks had been an established pattern; however, through our relocation and change of routine we had let that pattern slip away. We focused at first on the book, then were deterred by rainy West Coast weather. Later, the Christmas season had interfered. All of our excuses resulted in this unexpected hill where we found ourselves laboring on our walk. We didn't like it but it felt more like a setback than a wakeup call.

Our bodies didn't feel as healthy as when we had been walking regularly. Our mental and emotional well being had slipped too. We had days when we felt flat. To help me get back to the feeling level I needed to access for chapter five, we had watched tapes of Dr. Phil's Get Real Challenge from Oprah's television show. We had done a lot of release work and were feeling vulnerable.

The most significant part of writing chapter five was reliving the session with Father M. The memories and feelings that had surfaced were as painful as they had been before. I felt raw.

It hadn't been my intention to sequentially correlate each of the twelve steps to its corresponding chapter number, but here I was starting chapter six and thinking about step six – the enormity of my past and its impact on the balance of my life. I now find myself exactly where I'm supposed to be. I have to let go of it again.

Over the previous week there had been a lot of stuff percolating. I was unsettled, agitated, anxious and irritable. One day Kelly went birthday shopping with a friend. When she returned home that evening she noticed a marked shift in my personality. I was negative, fearful, questioning my writing ability. I beat myself up with the possibility that we were deluding ourselves and wasting our time on the book. Fortunately Kelly didn't take on my feelings. I went to bed. When I awoke, it was with the realization that I had slipped into the part of me that held my mother's fear-based perspective.

My slip back into the family roles didn't end there. Later that day we drove to the south end of the island to Victoria for BBQ pork with wontons in noodle soup, one of Chinatown's special treats. We followed this lunch with a visit to our favorite secondhand department store two blocks away. I found a couple of shirts to try on. As I was leaving the change room, I got into a confrontation with a store employee. I knew that I was doing it and there were people watching. It was embarrassing and it all happened so fast! I complained about the employee to the manager at the till. Finally, outside the store, I came face to face with the employee again. She had gone outside for a smoke break. We had further words, expanding our confrontation.

Kelly and I processed this behavior in the car. As we talked, we gradually understood that in the confrontation in the store, I had switched to my father's role, becoming irritable and abusive.

It was as if I was riding a pendulum; I had swung to one extreme the previous evening when I had played out my mom's stuff and now I had polarized back to my father's position. Our processing was not over my being unaccountable for my behavior; it was about understanding where the behavior had come from, why it had happened. Both of these mood swings are outside of my baseline behavior. Needless to say, I felt terrible. That feeling persisted. Part of me felt guilty and insisted that I owed the employee an apology, perhaps making an amend.

It's important to understand that the stuff from the past never completely goes away. It's not as conscious as something simmering on the back burner. It's more like it's back in the shadows somewhere. Usually, when I'm consciously taking care of myself and working my program, there aren't many embarrassing situations. In the twelve step programs we are warned to be especially careful on days when we become hungry, angry, lonely or tired. The acronym is H.A.L.T. For me, it seems important to add the word vulnerable to that list.

There are no quick fixes but behavior can be managed if you remain aware. The individual is responsible to maintain the health and emotional well being of that inner manager. He needs the time to respond rather than to react to life's situations.

In an effort to take better care of myself after my insightful step five with Father M., I decided to focus entirely on my therapy and codependency issues through attending meetings and doing workshops.

When I had been attending my large CoDA group for about a year, the group secretary was ready to resign. She had also served as a delegate representing our province at the annual CoDA conference in Arizona. She asked me if I would consider taking her place as the group secretary because she felt a conflict with holding both positions. I agreed. After going through the formalities, I assumed my new service position with the group.

Most of the CoDA meetings in the city had revolving chair people. This group was the exception. It was one of Canada's first meetings and it was large – most evenings there were more than a hundred people in attendance. There weren't many people who were willing to step into the leadership role. There were a lot of details on any given evening. The biggest challenge was finding breakout areas for the smaller groups after the opening speaker was finished.

I enjoyed the responsibility; the challenge was good for my self-esteem. In conjunction with this duty, I attended monthly inter-group meetings and became involved in the business of CoDA within the city. We had grown to about fifteen meetings in the greater Vancouver area and were approaching about thirty registered meetings throughout the province of British Columbia.

We held occasional dances and there was talk of organizing a convention for the groups in and around the city. I turned down an invitation to help organize the first convention because the commitment would have conflicted with my therapy time. I was still working occasionally for the bookstore and attending retreats. I was also attempting to build a relationship and was committed to the workbook twelve step study series.

Things were in flux, though. My relationship with Owen, the bookstore owner, had taken an unhealthy turn and was becoming toxic. We had a push-pull relationship; our communication level had deteriorated. I was unhappy with details in the preparatory work for my taping sessions and that sharp edge carried over to the retreats.

There was a new core group evolving and instead of putting in my former level of commitment, I was beginning to pull back. Everything has its time and a time to end. It was clear that I was moving in a different direction. It would have been good if I could have made a clean break and moved on in a good way, but I wasn't healthy enough to do it that way.

After I expressed some anger, Owen told me that some of the newcomers weren't feeling safe with my anger. He requested that I discontinue attending the retreats. That hurt; it was a painful parting. To make the parting complete, I severed my business connection with the bookstore.

In our group therapy, we had been discussing rebuilding relationships. It was important to distinguish between salvageable situations and toxic conditions. When I examined my relationship with Owen and the bookstore group, I assessed the hurt and damage compared to the level of feelings and commitment. The logical decision was to step back, do the grieving and move on. It was unlikely that the factors would change – a mutual effort to rebuild the relationship was not present.

This dictated a significant shift in my recovery program. I had recently ended my initial therapy processes with my first two therapists. Much like leaving AA to begin with ACOA, I was now leaving ACOA to focus on codependency issues in CoDA. The bookstore and the retreats had been pieces that did not fit into the new mosaic. The final scenes there spoke loudly of the need to make the change and showed that my focus needed to be on relationship recovery.

I concluded the workbook on the twelve steps with my *family group*. We were relieved to have completed it. For most of the group members it was a one-time commitment; after the six-month process we went our separate ways. Later, there were occasional chance encounters with group members, but for the most part we didn't attempt to maintain contact. I'm not sure whether that was about the content or depth of our sharing. I believe it was more about the forced intimacy that we had endured, much the same as what we had experienced in our family of origins. There were no Thanksgiving dinners or even Christmas cards between the members of our small family group.

I was still attempting to form a relationship with Jackie, my co-sponsor. When we had been seeing each other for several months, we decided to take our relationship to the next level. As her sister, Jillian, saw and felt the shift, she became hostile toward me. The push-pull aspect of the toxic triangle was now in full force. We each brought so much baggage into that relationship that our effort at intimacy was nothing less than heroic.

Jackie and I decided to become sexual. We made two unsuccessful attempts; one at my apartment and one at hers while Jillian was away at an evening class.

The sisters conferred and decided that blood is thicker than water. Jackie and Jillian had dumped their husbands in Los Angeles, sold their household contents and moved to Vancouver together. Who was I to come between them?

Jackie and I had a final argument while sitting in my car in the parking lot across from her apartment. I made the decision – I told her to get out. That was it. I drove home, cold and numb. I kept hearing the words coming from my mouth, "get out, get out, get out!"

My grief over the loss of that relationship wasn't as bad as I had anticipated that it would be. The loneliness wasn't as intense as expected either. It added to my understanding of time alone versus loneliness. As an only child, I grew up learning to amuse myself, to do everything by myself. After the break-up of my near relationship, I rather enjoyed my solitude. I had never before had an in-depth, intimate relationship with a peer in my life. The concept of loneliness was not something I feared. I got all the superficial contact I needed by attending meetings or going for coffee in a group after meetings.

I began to meet new people without ever really going out on a date. Several times women asked me to accompany them to events. Sometimes we had fun and the evenings were successful; other times I felt threatened or trapped and I was relieved to get away. As I learned how women felt, I wasn't particularly ready to enter another friendship or relationship.

Gradually I felt stronger about myself and people gave me supportive feedback about the subsequent changes they saw in me. It was 1989 and I had been working on myself for over three years. I explored the option of returning to work. I talked about this in therapy. It would be a big step. Everyone in my group and my therapist thought it was a good idea. No one was telling me to do it. It was my idea and my decision.

My therapist suggested that it might be wise idea to find some sort of work in a minor capacity in my old profession. This was so that I could continue to emphasize my recovery process and growth rather than to completely abandon everything to focus on a new career. I had mixed reactions to this. I understood the logic of his recommendation but I didn't want to go back to another golf course.

As January of 1990 approached, I warmed to the idea of starting a new decade with a new goal. I was in my power and had enough positive energy to create something new for myself. I enrolled in a job reentry program at the YMCA where I spent the holidays getting ready for work. I focused on letting go of the "unemployable" label that had been stamped on my file by the welfare ministry

My experience at the YMCA was different than I had anticipated. I had neither worked at a regular job for four years nor had I been around people who were not in recovery. Considerable adjustments had to be made in my social attitudes. I was out of balance and had a difficult time not preaching my recovery position. It was a humbling experience; a step-by-step confidence and esteem building program. I attended all the sessions, co-operated to the best of my ability and fulfilled the assigned requirements.

I applied for a position installing sprinkler systems in commercial and residential applications – a variation of work I had done on the golf course. I got the job. The owner of the company had grander designs and pushed me to become his assistant. I had no knowledge of the scope of his applications and I was faced with unfamiliar codes, regulations, estimating and design modification. As a precision person, I worked at my own speed and, because of my private golf course experience, demanded a high level of performance from the staff. I didn't fit the company and was unable to make the adjustment. The owner fired me in favor of a young highballer who had been hired at the same time I was. It was a setback. I cried. I returned to the program at the YMCA.

I then attempted to create a job for myself at an addiction research and education agency. I spent hours writing a proposal and creating a job description. I even included a plausible way of generating enough income to cover my salary. I knew the director vaguely from audio taping plenary sessions for him during conferences that he had sponsored. I set up an appointment to present my proposal to him. He politely listened to me and then he informed me that he couldn't hire me; there was no time, direction or budget to support my proposal. He did it nicely.

That put me back at the YMCA. Spring was approaching and I was getting discouraged. I had several run-ins with a user-unfriendly computer. I got frustrated as it seemed to keep deleting my work. The computer became a symbol for my incompatibility with the work world. Just when I was about to throw in the towel, one of the group members brought me a newspaper clipping from a weekly community newspaper. The district parks department was advertising for someone with experience operating tractors and gang mowers. I knew the basics so I jumped at the opportunity.

I delivered two separate cover letters and letters of application – one to the main office as directed in the advertisement and another to the superintendent's office in the public works department. I interviewed and successfully landed the full-time position at an attractive union hourly rate. The work was seasonal with the option of permanent employment.

Having survived the probation period, I became a temporary, full-time employee and union member. I worked by myself using either the seven-gang mower to maintain the large athletic fields in the city or I used a smaller three-gang unit and cut the grass in dozens of small parks and playgrounds. I loved the work. It was demanding and challenging. I had the freedom to set my own work schedule and was able to take the time to do a good job. I had loved cutting fairways on the golf courses, particularly making patterns on the grass by mowing in different directions to crosscut the turf. I expressed my creativity and exercised my attention to detail. My work was appreciated and I got favorable feedback from my supervisors. From time to time, I contributed my technical knowledge on specific applications such as over-seeding and top dressing. I was initially happy.

The most difficult adjustment was to the social and political environment among the work crews. The ambient male energy was anger, boredom and complacency. I could distance from this for the most part because my job allowed me to work alone. However, I came into contact with the entire crew and the various departments when arriving in the morning and leaving work at the end of the day. I also had to work with them or around them at different times during the season. Gradually I took on their negativity like a cancer. Once started, it spread within me.

When the grass stopped growing in the fall and the ground became too soft for equipment, I joined small crews for cleanup and construction projects. My co-workers ranged from the cocky young kids who bragged endlessly about their latest exploits and drinking binges to the older married men who were depressed, frustrated and bored.

I was happy to be laid off from the parks department crew close to Christmas. I looked forward to spending time walking the sea wall, reading and focusing on my recovery program.

I now had my own apartment and had started furnishing it. Actually this had been an experience in itself. While I had been enrolled at the YMCA program, my relationship with my apartment landlady deteriorated. When I had moved into that two-bedroom apartment, my landlady was rarely home so I had the place to myself much of the time. She worked in Vancouver and operated a small business at her daughter's place south of the city. Gradually she had spent more and more time at our shared home. Our personalities and lifestyles began to conflict. Just after I started with the parks department, we had a huge blow up and I moved out. I found another shared accommodation situation, in a house this time, but it didn't work out either. By the end of that summer I was again searching for alternate accommodation. A woman I knew and respected asked if I wanted to share her two-bedroom place with her and her cats. This move didn't last for one week. We still liked each other but we quickly discovered that we couldn't live together.

I found an older apartment at a low monthly rate. I had no furniture, dishes or anything. To furnish it, I discovered it was fun to secondhand shop. By my winter lay-off, I had the place comfortably fitted out. I was over forty years of age and for the first time I felt at home. Although it wasn't fancy, I enjoyed coming home to my own cozy apartment.

My building manager was an extremely abusive rager. There was a steady stream of renters coming and going because of his temper tantrums and underhanded policies. I knew to give him plenty of space and began to ask myself why I continued to attract raging men into my life. I recognized the precariousness of my situation. Angry men at work, angry men at home, angry father, angry Ted.

That winter I focused on the twelve-step workbook study and my other recovery modalities. Even though I was using the same workbook and answering the identical set of questions, I was having a completely different experience this time. The people in my small family group were each unique and every one of us brought our particular baggage together in a new way. The dynamics were relative; I found different parts of my past being revealed to me as we progressed through the steps.

My workshop experiences were changing for me as well. I attended major workshops with John Bradshaw and Terry Kellogg. Although these experiences were important for me and I benefited from attending, I was aware of a shift in my attitude about them. They took on an educational aspect as much as a therapeutic appeal but I noticed that I wasn't as prone to placing the teachers on a pedestal, as I had been earlier in my healing journey. Moreover, I recognized that I was attending these events in a social capacity and my ego was as concerned with being seen as I was in exposing my past. My role seemed to be changing once more.

At the John Bradshaw workshop, I drew attention to myself by volunteering to read a poem I wrote during one of the sessions. It was definitely a moment of "look at me and how well I'm doing."

At the Kellogg workshop, I found myself doing two things. First, I attempted to impress him and his partner, Marval, with my knowledge of the information he had presented in his book *Broken Toys, Broken Dreams*. This had been one of the most significant books in my self-education. They remarked that I seemed to have done my homework. I then challenged that he made no reference to CoDA in the resource appendix to his book. Instead he advised readers to attend Alanon. In my naivety, I offered him the address of CoDA in Arizona. He politely refused and spoke about the benefits of attending Alanon. I recognized that I was beginning to challenge authority.

Conflict was still coming up for me. One of the things that I had learned about myself in therapy was my pattern of setting up conflict, engaging and then either continuing in the relationship or cutting off. I needed conflict in order to create intimacy. This pattern became apparent everywhere I turned. I was really getting tired of the chaos; I needed a new life strategy.

My therapist advised me that boring was good; it was the opposite of what I had been creating everywhere I went. Boring is safe, boring is serene, boring is predictable and boring is healthy. Look for the boring, bask in the boring and learn to develop the boring in everything. This was to be my new focus. Stop doing, stop running around, stop the busyness, stop the conflict and stop the chaos.

It's easier to grasp a new focus than it is to put it in place. I had been consistently told to view these changes as habits – that it takes about thirty days of diligent practice to successfully develop a new habit. This seemed like a major life change. I knew that when people faced stress or compromising situations they tended to revert to old behavior. I didn't want to be defeatist so I allowed for the possibility that this shift could happen for me. My usual manner of dealing with this kind of change was to exercise control, control and control. I was prone to setting up control cycles and, when things got rough, I would swing to the extreme and release, release, release (i.e. fall back to old habits or binge; this was particularly true for my eating habits).

I needed a greater level of spiritual help to make it through this seemingly overwhelming hurdle. I maintained that native people have a greater spiritual connection with themselves and with the planet earth. I bought and studied an excellent book called *Dancing With the Wheel* by a Seattle elder named Sun Bear.

Then, another situation cast me into major chaos. This had to do with the large CoDA meeting I was chairing at the church across the city. The church was a high-energy congregation and was connected to a group led by a recovering alcoholic based out of Detroit. The ministers were skilled motivational speakers who had been attending CoDA meetings as well as providing the premises to us. Without any prior warning, they gave us one-month notice to vacate their building and find a new location for our meeting.

They didn't even kick us out in person. Instead they took the easy route of sending the notice with a member of the congregation who was also attending CoDA meetings. They had been directed by the leader from Detroit to evict us. We were told that the church had formed a partnership with a group from Quebec who had a treatment center for codependency in the Laurentian Mountains. Recovery for pay had broad sided us. I was crushed. There was no discussion – just the absolute directive.

The group members rallied. We located a suitable replacement site for the meeting but the damage had been done. The anger, betrayal and violation took its toll. The meeting size dwindled to half and then dropped lower as the change in venue took place. The sterility of the new site at a hospital and the aloofness of the bureaucrats that ran it contributed to the attrition. I became part of that attrition. After the meeting stabilized, I stepped down from my position as chairperson and stopped attending.

That spring, the first CoDA convention for the Vancouver inter-group was held in the Fraser Valley. The successful event aroused a yearning within me. The chairperson for the event, Marilyn K., had been our first delegate to attend the World Service Conference for CoDA that was held each September in Phoenix, Arizona. She had invited the executive director of the business office for CoDA, Carmen P., to attend the convention as the keynote speaker. I was impressed with Carmen's talk and intrigued by the concept of world service. In fact, I was envious and wanted to be involved at that level. I rationalized that it would be beneficial to my recovery process by providing me with a goal to which I could aspire. I've heard it said: be careful what you wish for because you might get it.

Putting these lofty ideas out of my mind, I settled into a new season of parks work. Things were about the same. Management was happy with my work. The foreman commended me for my ability to work without supervision and to take the initiative to correct the things that needed to be done without direction. He expanded my responsibilities and that did not sit well with my coworkers.

Because it was a union position, I came under attack for carrying a workload that normally two or three people would perform. Unable to deal with the conflict, I referred the angry workers to talk it out with management. I felt justified in my efforts. However, the end result for me was a further sense of ostracism. All the stuff about being different came up for me once again. I was doing well, acting with integrity, but I was in conflict. I still wasn't getting that the conflict was the co-workers stuff - not mine. I took on their rejection and didn't feel safe.

It was a challenge for me to be around people who weren't in recovery. I was used to conflict and minor disagreements but nothing compared to the lack of safety and shame that there was something critically the matter with me. I had an underlying sense of anger, hostility and aggression that permeated my life in the real world. I felt it in traffic, in retail establishments and here it was again, at my place of work. I witnessed threats and acts of violence on a daily basis. I felt threatened and fearful when getting up to go to work. I did okay when I was one-on-one with people but there was a decided shift in my perception, a feeling of unsafety, in a group.

I was called into the deputy superintendent's office. It felt like being called to the vice principal's office back in school. I was not chastised and my fears were unfounded. Instead my work was praised and I was offered a promotion to a permanent, full-time position. Management acknowledged that I was in recovery and allowed me leeway to attend workshops and other events important to my process. I consented to take the pledge of allegiance to the Queen and made the transition to my new status as a permanent government employee.

My quick ascent through the ranks further distanced me from my coworkers. The norm was to work for four or five years in the seasonal capacity before being offered a permanent position. I isolated and put my effort into my job performance.

My work ethic and performance had also been recognized on another level and this time it was within the bounds of my recovery program. I was asked by the British Columbia delegate to the world service conference of CoDA in Phoenix to run for election for the position of second delegate. Each area was allowed two delegates and two alternates. I was pleased with this affirmation and consented to let my name stand. I was elected to the position and two acquaintances that I had performed service work with were elected as alternates. This meant that four of us would be attending conference in Phoenix in September. We eagerly anticipated this opportunity.

My therapist was supportive and helped me to acknowledge the recognition that I was receiving in both the workplace and in my recovery group. We discussed the possibility that it was okay to succeed in life and that I no longer had to remain loyal to my legacy of devolution. It was okay to surpass the experience of my parents and ask for what I wanted in life. We began to examine my tendency to sabotage success and to victimize myself.

Finally, September arrived and it was time to travel to Arizona. I had always dreamed of going to the desert and I looked forward to the heat. Sun always energized me. I was like the small town kid in the big city. Everything took on an exaggerated proportion. I had read about the founders, trustees and world service in AA literature. Now here I was meeting their counterparts in a different twelve-step organization. I was awed and overwhelmed.

Having been asked to choose which committee I would serve on, I was unprepared for the initial commitment to one of the eight or nine options available. I needed time to think. The evening before the conference began I joined a group of people in the hot tub by the pool. To my amazement I began to meet the major players at the conference. One by one, I met the trustees and learned about the committees. Then to my amazement, I met the founders, Ken and Mary R.. All this while at the hot tub.

This definitely was a higher power situation. I had asked for help in deciding which committee to join. Before I realized what had happened I had met all these people. I easily made my decision and participated in the three full days of business. It was warm early in Phoenix and I was up and in the pool by six each morning. I attended sessions throughout the day and enjoyed the entertainment each evening. I was energized and usually one of the last to leave the hot tub every evening.

All the retreats and meetings and workshops had served me well. I enjoyed meeting people in recovery and was impressed by the level of growth I witnessed. I was also touched by the openness and friendliness that was extended to me. To date, this was the pinnacle of my efforts and I reveled in it. I dismissed the rumors of dissension that were whispered in alcoves and behind closed doors around the courtyard and pool.

Hard politics had been in play and a decision had been made to delete the paid position of executive director from the business office. I heard the rumblings about the location of world service and its possible conflict with the U.S. level of service.

The four of us returned to Canada, happy and firm in our resolve to act as a team in our stewardship of the recovery group in our corner of the world. We also decided to unite our talents as executive members and organize a provincial convention for the next spring. Further, we envisioned a Canadian convention and discussed the possibility of hosting a world convention several years down the road.

I was eager to share my excitement first with my home group. The news was well received and the energy began to ripple outward as we began a recruitment process to attract people to our convention committee. The response was different at my therapy group.

Conflict took one final torpedo shot at me before I made the conscious decision to embrace boringness as a way of life, working to reduce and eliminate chaos from my life. The conflict this time arose between my therapist and myself. We had worked through endless issues to form a therapeutic relationship. Most of the issues had dissolved in the alchemy of process but there were several issues of trust that had never been resolved.

While I was away in Arizona, my therapist had disbanded the therapy group session that I had been a part of for over two years. His reason was that the group had grown stagnant and he wanted to shift the evening focus to new groups for couples dealing with relationship problems. I understood what he was saying and I could see how important this new format was for him and for the people who needed that work. But I was pissed because I wasn't in a relationship and couldn't be included. I projected my old resentments about leaving my last therapy situation in a similar manner.

We met to talk about the situation. It didn't go well. I challenged him and let him know that I felt completely betrayed by his process and my lack of opportunity to participate in the decision. I wasn't buying the fact that it was ultimately his choice.

He guaranteed me that I could continue individual therapy. My parents had cut off their financial support when I had begun work. However, as a demonstration of good faith, he offered me a full year of free therapy if I chose to continue. I was too emotional, hurt and reactive. I couldn't hear what he had to say and turned down his generous proposal. I chose to run away and feel sorry for myself. I blurted out an inappropriate comment about what a shitty way to end a relationship and bolted from his office.

I have neither seen nor heard from this gentle man since. He had been a therapist, a mentor and a friend. I hope to change that and I trust that the opportunity will present itself. Better still, I will reconnect with him in some form of amend process.

As the realization of my reactive behavior hit home, the high level of energy I had experienced on my return from Arizona diminished. At work, I was once again relegated to small crews. Unhappiness and melancholy eroded my sense of well being. Another grieving process was initiated and my life slowed down. I hadn't reached the level of boring but that new image was etched into my belief system. Some things come slower than others; everything comes in its own time.

Shifts seem to happen when the time is ripe. I reasoned that if I had been in a relationship I could have continued with the therapy group. That led me to conclude that the universe was giving me a message. I considered that it would be nice to attempt another relationship but I had no idea of how or when that would come. I was just another single person in relationship recovery talking about my recovery process, like an armchair athlete watching the game from a vantage point of relative safety. Likewise, I saw a lot of people approaching recovery through the relative ease of observer. I knew that it was time for me to step into the real work – going through recovery issues with a partner in a relationship.

I had to reevaluate my process and look at how far I had come. I had been a pitiful drunk on the verge of suicide. Gradually I had entered recovery, become abstinent, developed a support system and program of recovery and accepted the notion of a higher power in my life. I had done considerable introspection and participated in therapy. Change was ongoing and I was growing. I envisioned that my next step was to take an active part in relationship recovery by finding a partner or having a partner find me.

I was only half way through the process that I wished to experience.

As this chapter comes to an end it is without a doubt symbolic of the halfway point of the book. I had, to this point, simply been acquiring the tools with which to begin to build my new life. I would need to add new tools to enter a new phase of my life, a phase more challenging and rewarding than anything I had encountered to date.

This week I returned to the secondhand department store. I asked my higher power for help. There was a parking place directly in front and the employee I'd had conflict with was working. I shopped then met her in her corner of the store. I apologized and made an amend. So did she. Both of us had felt badly and both of us were relieved to have an opportunity to heal the situation. I leave this chapter feeling much better than I did when it began.

Chapter Seven

Addicted to Busyness

It's been a couple of weeks since I sat at my table and allowed the words to flow. I've faced considerable resistance to start again. Yesterday I attempted to begin but, after several hours of frustration, found something else to do.

My first week away from the book was a celebratory time. We had guests from the city. We visited, played cards, cooked fine meals and shared intimate conversation in front of the fire while being serenaded by soothing music.

The visits were followed by a snowstorm. Our world transformed into the idealized country winter wonderland that lives in every person's mind. The snow fell wet, heavy and deep. Amid the activity and external transformation, I lost my connection to spirit. Fear, worry and doubt stormed in my head. They drifted through the pastures of my brain leaving me stranded and alone.

Over the last several days, the snow changed to rain and the whiteness melted down to recognizable forms. Coincidentally, my dark mood gradually melted. The anger subsided and the urge to continue my story re-emerged.

Peering through the foggy rain, I can again distinguish the trees across the lake. They are lined up along the shore, peering into the depths like a crowd gathering to glimpse an unknown horror at an accident scene. Their silent witness takes me back to the guilt and dishonor of my own character defects.

Guilt is good. Guilt can be released. Shame is the bind that distorts truth and beauty. Shame causes all forms of deviant behavior.

It's humbling to be back into the stuff. Humility is the quality needed for the next part of this process. In step seven, we are required to humbly ask our higher power to remove our shortcomings.

To focus only on life's transgressions is unhealthy. That obsession may become a form of pride that blocks progress. On this healing journey, there is a constant give and take – two steps forward, and one back. Eventually the burden of the past is released and life can be lived, not merely endured.

With this mixture of feelings, I recall my life in the early 1990's. I had just completed six months of steady employment in the parks department and I was exhausted. As a permanent employee, I no longer had the option of a seasonal layoff to recuperate. I felt trapped working in close confines with un-recovered people.

I was no longer in therapy but continued to participate in a group on the twelve steps workbook. I also remained loyal to my CoDA home group and attended regularly. Both of these meetings were vital to my process by providing me with spiritual connection, fellowship and a sense of belonging to something important. I was now part of the solution instead of being part of the problem. That simple belief kept me going.

Service work also contributed in a major way. People said that working the steps was a greedy program; the more effort expended, the greater the result. In high school I'd heard some kids say that those who were greedy would get more. Desperate to recover, I was willing to go to any lengths so I embraced this form of greed. I figured that the more effort I put into service work, the greater my benefits and rewards would be. That should translate directly into the healing I would experience.

I had been elected to serve as a CoDA delegate representing my province. In accordance with the twelve concepts of world service, I committed to understanding and performing my duties at that level. I was required to mail regular written reports to my committee chairperson and to participate in conference calls, correspondence and maintaining connection to a different level of business. My function as delegate was to have all the necessary work completed by September in time for the annual service conference.

There were also a variety of local duties. My name and phone number were published in the provincial newsletter and there were always phone calls from people who were interested in starting home groups in their area. While most of the calls were enthusiastic and supportive, others were political, negative and not nice. I was learning to take the good with the bad.

We formed a committee to organize the provincial convention to be held the following spring. We met once a month to co-ordinate our efforts. As chairperson and convention emcee, I felt secure that I had the skills to execute these responsibilities. I was learning diplomacy and cooperation. This wasn't about power and control; it was about using my leadership skills and delegating responsibility. I was developing a sense of responsibility and requiring a new degree of humility.

I was happy to have the service work as an avenue to direct my interest and energy. It was a medicine of sorts when compared to the contamination in my place of employment.

I missed my therapy group so I joined another step study group in order to have a place to share my stuff. I had begun to internalize a lot of the negativity and stress from work. It was hard not to isolate and envision catastrophe.

By Halloween, I needed a workshop. That came in the form of a yearly CoDA retreat in Squamish, a town on the highway north between Vancouver and Whistler. That weekend was organized by the other new delegate to the annual CoDA world service conference. Each year, about fifty people attended this workshop. It was a lot of fun. There was an indoor swimming pool, acreage along the river for eagle spotting, activity rooms and a large front room with a huge stone fireplace. An annual costume dress-up was part of the weekend's events.

One thing out of the ordinary happened at the Squamish workshop. Late on the first evening, I was sitting with an alternate delegate folding newsletters near the fire when we were joined by two women. They couldn't sleep and wanted to share the fire. One of the ladies had just moved to Vancouver. I invited her to attend my home group and gave her my phone number. Her name was Kelly.

Yes, this lady was to become my wife. This is the boy meets girl part of the book. On reflection, this is another pivotal point in my recovery.

Kelly called me in early December and we set up our first outing to a huge event at the convention center. That day featured internationally recognized speakers including Louise Hay, Shakti Gawain and Deepak Chopra. We arrived at the Pan Pacific Hotel earlier than the other fifteen hundred participants. While we shared an excellent breakfast, we asked our higher power for tickets and good seats.

In the hotel lobby, we met a person who gave us her tickets for half price. "Good start," we thought. As we entered the packed convention center, we wandered down the aisle toward the front. There didn't appear to be seats anywhere. Suddenly a woman asked us if we needed seats. She led us to a roped off section at the front that was reserved for speakers and VIPs. Louise Hay was sitting directly in front of us.

Our higher power had led us at the perfect time, to the right place to get the best seats in the house. That magical moment was the beginning of our friendship. We enjoyed the entire day and took new concepts home with us. One speaker said that spirituality is simply the connection between people – like the new connection between Kelly and me.

Neither Kelly nor I viewed each other as relationship material. From that position of safety we decided to develop a friendship. She was recently out of a relationship and was in the process of developing a friendship with her roommate. The roommate and I didn't feel comfortable together and it seemed like the beginning of another triangle. I decided to give the roommate full distance and agreed to attempt to develop a simple friendship with Kelly. It was good to have someone to talk things over with. Kelly and I began talking on the phone frequently and walking the sea wall on weekends.

That January we joined a group celebration at the old Expo Pavilion to contribute to the shifting consciousness of the planet earth. This event was known as the eleven-eleven – represented as 11:11. It was a spiritually significant global happening and was celebrated simultaneously by groups around the world. The theory was that if enough people around the world participated this would initiate a harmonic shift in planetary consciousness affecting dualism, cause and effect and polarity. We didn't understand much of what was going on but we had a yearning for things spiritual. For me, it was making the decision to be part of the solution.

By the springtime, Kelly realized that she couldn't live with that roommate any longer. Together we found her an apartment in a downtown area of Vancouver called the West End, two blocks from the sea wall. We began to walk together more frequently. We discovered that we shared many things in common: a commitment to recovery and spiritual growth, a love of food, music and dancing and a desire to travel and spend time in the sun at the beach.

Our mutual passion for food meant we were always ready to try different restaurants. We both loved ethnic soups. That developed into a routine of going out for soup. We particularly coveted Asian ramen, udon, hot and sour and noodle soups. Sharing soup was a great ending to rainy winter walks.

I had learned some of the basics of Italian cooking from my previous lady friend and began enjoying cooking and experimenting with pasta dishes. I don't know where my interest in food originated as my background is Irish on my father's side and Swedish on my mother's. Kelly's broad ethnic background was a natural for eclectic food habits: Irish and Italian on her mother's side, French and Cree Indian on her father's. That dubbed her Mètis. Her mother's family recipe for spaghetti and meatballs exceeds anything I have ever tasted.

That spring was a busy time – the busyness distracted me from conditions at my work place that were growing intolerable. Instead I focused on organizing details of the provincial CoDA convention.

We had confirmed that a woman from Phoenix would be our keynote speaker. Annie D. was one of the first people to join CoDA and had an outgoing personality. We all looked forward to what she would bring to our area. The committee had worked hard and put together an outstanding program with lots of options.

The convention went without a hitch and everyone proclaimed it to be a success. As a committee within the home group, we decided to continue to work together and made plans to host the first Canadian convention the following spring. We asked CoDA founders, Ken and Mary R., to be our keynote speakers. One further piece that we hoped to put in place was a national service level for CoDA in Canada. Preparations were developed to invite interested delegates from all the provinces and territories to attend a service conference prior to the convention.

When the provincial convention ended and people returned home, I was left with a sense of loneliness and loss. Kelly had been working with at-risk youth. She was away for the summer as part of a team that was setting up a wilderness camp for teens.

My step group had ended and I no longer had close connections with people from my home group. I didn't have the energy to find a new therapist. It felt like it would take too much time and effort to develop the intimacy I needed to talk about the depth of my despair; it just sat there - internalized and percolating.

The helplessness of my work situation escalated and I felt vulnerable wherever I went. Gassing up and washing the car was a chore; shopping was a strain; even going to the beach and lying in the sun was no longer any fun. The sea wall was my only release. I pounded around the perimeter of Stanley Park – angry and reactive.

My work situation deteriorated. I was isolated and seldom smiled. Instead of enjoying the summer evenings, I simply went home and lay on the couch. My chronic depression spiraled down and suicidal thinking patterns reemerged. I was desperate. I couldn't stand to even hear the telephone ring.

The first weekend in August I noticed an advertisement for a native pow wow on the Capilano Reserve near Lion's Gate Bridge. I still maintained an attraction for native spirituality and decided to attend.

At the pow wow, hundreds of people gathered. When the drumming began and the grand entry procession started, I felt both hypnotized and connected. I watched one particular traditional dancer with fascination. The color of his regalia, the fur, the feathers and red felt spoke to me on a level that I cannot consciously recall ever experiencing before. There was an expanding feeling and pressure in my breastbone. After the opening ceremony I talked to that dancer and told him about the sensation I had experienced. He shared that he'd had the identical experience at a pow wow when he was a child. His confirmation reinforced my sense of connection and specialness.

As the weekend unfolded, I talked to several people I had met at various events over the years. There was a group of about ten people at the pow wow who were preparing to go into the mountains for a vision quest. One of them suggested that I go along; perhaps I could find some answers to my recent dilemma. After a brief interview with the elder who was to lead the group, he consented to allow me to participate.

118

To prepare for my vision quest, I had a lot of things to do in a very short time frame. I had to buy tobacco, yarn and red and white material from the fabric shop. A woman instructed me in the art of making my tobacco ties, which I needed for protection on the mountain.

I couldn't get hold of my boss so I left a note on his door saying that I would be away for a week. I then forgot the world as I knew it and began the process of rituals, cleansing and preparation for the quest. This included prayers, fasting, a sweat lodge and baths in the pools of the Seymour River.

We traveled into the coastal mountains to a traditional area near Lillooet. There we gathered for a special teaching. We received instruction on how to talk to spirit, how to communicate with wildlife, including mosquitoes, which we asked to help us achieve our purpose. We learned traditional secrets on how to wipe ourselves down with green plants to prevent the bugs from eating us alive. During the vision quest, we would be visited daily by the elder for teachings and support.

After a final pipe ceremony, just as darkness fell we were each taken by the native elder to our individual spots on the mountain. We were to spend four days and nights on that mountain by ourselves. There was no time to set up a camp or anything. No food. No water. No sleep. It happened so quickly. One moment I was part of a group, the next I was alone with nothing but one blanket and the clothes on my back. I had no matches, no water, no watch – nothing. There was only me in the darkness.

The mosquitoes knew I was there and went crazy over me. I forced myself to ask the mosquitoes to help me, to only bite me if they saw me falling asleep, and I explained to them the spiritual purpose that I was undergoing. I also explained this to the trees and plants and asked permission to take leaves to wash my skin and add protection from the insects.

My eyes adjusted to the night. In the clear sky, more stars were visible than I had ever seen before. I eventually discerned shapes in the darkness and eventually saw to a limited degree. I located a stump about knee high and approximately a foot in diameter. A broken tree trunk about three or four inches in diameter made a basic staff. I spent each of the four nights standing on the stump supporting myself with the staff. If I fell asleep I would fall off the stump and wake up. I kept a small pebble under my tongue to help me salivate and moisten my mouth.

I could write an entire book about my time on the mountain. I trusted in my tobacco ties which I had hung in the trees as directed by my elder, War Dance. I felt the protection of nature.

Each day the elder showed me where the caribou had bedded down near me the previous evening, content to listen to me sing, whistle or simply ramble on as I did everything conceivable to stay awake. He taught me about the evolution of nature and how to recognize different aspects from my immediate environment.

After a slight rain on the third night, I found myself licking water drops off grass blades. It was not enough to drink, only enough to moisten my parched mouth.

Each day I explored my section of the mountain. I discovered where the bear had ripped open rotting tree trunks or the various other wildlife had left their marks. Each evening I stood on my stump, and faced the four directions and prayed and meditated. The coyotes in the distance and I listened to each other.

At first I didn't like my spot. After fuming and fussing about how unfair it was that others had better spots, as the days passed and as I began to understand the process of nature, my spot became beautiful. Certain trees were like company. In places they grew in bunches that looked like families. I recognized the shapes and shadows in the night that recurred in their identical positions each evening. They took on specific forms for me.

The last morning's daybreak was as spectacular and colorful as any sunset I have ever seen. By this time the mosquitoes had long passed any interest in the smell of my blood. By nine o'clock in the morning, I was barefoot and dressed only in my shorts, rolling in the long grass near my stump like a dog on his back. The feeling of at-oneness with my surroundings was such that I have never experienced before or since.

We returned by car caravan to our sweat lodge at the native reserve near the river. On the drive back, I identified the faces of the Grandfathers in the rock formations. Now I understood why the cliff near Squamish was called the Chief.

We drank a cleansing tea, went through another sweat lodge ceremony and bathed in the river. Then each of us told our experience to a group of elders who interpreted our signs and happenings for us. We had an ending feast and then returned to our homes to sleep.

Part of the teachings and interpretations that I received were similar to what I had learned in therapy. Most spoke to my need for empowerment and spiritual connection. The elders suggested that my teachings weren't over – more would be revealed in the months and years to come, particularly about the shadow images.

I returned to work to discover that my supervisor hadn't received my note and everyone had wondered what had happened to me. I had missed a week's work without notice. However, because there was no prior pattern to my absenteeism, I was mildly reprimanded and the day-to-day routine resumed.

As September came, I was preparing to go to Phoenix when I was once again called into the parks department deputy superintendent's office. I approached the meeting with nervousness, fearing that it had to do with my missed time or my obvious estrangement from my co-workers. Instead I was asked to attend a managers' workshop that conflicted with my departure time for Phoenix. When I brought up the scheduling conflict, to my surprise the superintendent supported my recovery commitment. He asked simply that I attend as much of the workshop as possible before I needed to leave for the airport.

On arrival in Phoenix, I had a certain amount of anxiety — some mixed emotions around employment and some because I had an agenda going into the conference. It was good to reconnect with the acquaintances and people I had worked with in the past. It was nice to see new faces and I anticipated the opening of the session with excitement. Right away, politics raised their ugly head. A committee petitioned the conference that only the U.S. delegates should have a vote; Canadians or delegates from other countries could only participate as observers. As Canadians were the only international delegates present, this was aimed at us.

I went cold and numb. I asked my higher power for help. I got permission to address the delegates. I don't really remember what I said and it doesn't matter now. My statement had to do with the fact that people around the globe needed a CoDA world service base. They needed to belong to an inclusive, not exclusive, organization. It was unfair that this group that had historically served all countries now was intending to only serve people in recovery from the United States.

When I finished the delegates began to clap. Then they stood up and they kept clapping. I was receiving a standing ovation! It still brings tears to my eyes. Me – a standing ovation! I have never felt that level of acceptance or achievement at any other time in my life. A vote was taken on the issue. The motion was denied and CoDA USA continued to be a conference for people in recovery all over the world.

The next new business dealt with elections of replacements for the trustees who made up the board. Delegates had previously submitted applications and resumes putting their names up as new trustees. Mine was included. Mine was voted down. Then it was coffee time. Not one of the over one hundred people in the room would make eye contact with me.

Moments earlier I had received a standing ovation and pats on the back. Now I was invisible. This was probably the greatest mood swing I had ever experienced. In less than an hour I went from the peak of acceptance to the valley of rejection. Somehow I endured. I had three full days of business to participate in. I survived the ride on the emotional roller coaster, and with the help of our small delegation, successfully negotiated the privilege to host the next world convention in two years time. Then, we persuaded the founders to speak at our first Canadian convention to be held the following spring.

This is the fun part of service work. We were learning to perform the demands of business within a relatively safe system. We learned that it was okay to be real and openly express our full range of emotions. We received support and encouragement for our efforts. The benefit of this experience tempered us for life in the real world and provided us with a vision of how things could be.

This part of my journey was rich, rewarding and full of energy. It flowed. I felt empowered, vital and proud to be making a significant contribution to my twelve step organization. I was learning what it felt like to be successful.

We returned home proud of our accomplishments and with renewed energy to spark our convention committees. I had received personal encouragement from Ken and Mary R. and other trustees to pursue my vision of becoming a trustee on the board of directors.

At the same time I had conflicted feelings because I wasn't congruent in all areas of my life. I wasn't in a love relationship but I was developing a friendship. I was extremely unhappy in the work place, yet I was being groomed for management.

I returned to work – that other world, the real world. Things weren't the same there. The energy, the happiness, and the sense of worth in doing important work was missing. It was just a job with the rainy season fast approaching. This signaled the return to small work crews, teaming up with the cocky younger workers and the complacent older ones. I couldn't maintain my personal power in these situations. The sense of being trapped returned. My energy drained away and I began to slip into unhappiness and depression. My day job wasn't working for me. I felt stuck, unappreciated and confined. This was not the work I wanted to be doing or the daily life I wanted to be living.

Fortunately, Kelly had returned from her summer's ordeal at camp. She had been the only adult survivor from her house group. All the other workers had either left or suffered burnout. She had been pushed to the edge and her strength shone through. She had maintained her power. In fact, she had been promoted to house head.

We both were unhappy with our work situations but from different perspectives. I was fourteen years older than Kelly. Retirement benefits dangled like a carrot on a stick for this mule. I was in fear-based thinking and was contemplating slow death through employment. The big compromise, the path that my father had taken, could be called either the path of least resistance or the path of disease manifestation. Was I to become a clone of my father, another Archie Bunker? There was no way I could continue for another seventeen years in this agony.

Kelly spoke the unspeakable "Quit!"

I couldn't be patient with it. As the rainy season began, every minor annoyance was amplified out of proportion. To add insult to injury, I had been sent to an ear specialist when I failed a routine hearing test required of all employees. I learned that I had lost over fifty percent of the hearing in each ear, leaving me about forty-five percent hearing. The loss was in the low frequency range of sounds. The audiologist advised that a hearing aid would do nothing for my particular type of hearing loss.

Further, my lungs were congested and I had developed a chronic cough similar to the smoker's hack. My doctor diagnosed it as having been caused by inhaling excessive diesel fumes from the leaky exhaust pipe on my work tractor. There was also a good chance that these fumes were causing problems with my mental health as well. The union wasn't prepared to help me on a claim; both the union and management scorned the notion that inhaled exhaust fumes could be that physically or mentally harmful.

I heeded Kelly's counsel and wrote a letter of resignation, making it effective immediately. My last day's work was completed without the usual two weeks notice. I had to act that quickly. Something inside said that if I waited, like the union advised, I would submit, compromise and sign on for the balance of my employment sentence with the faint glow of retirement too far down the tunnel of the future to matter.

That was a Friday. Directly after cleaning out my stuff from the change room at work, I drove up to Squamish to participate in our annual Halloween retreat. It was important for me to be surrounded by supportive people. My melancholy and depression magically diminished as I processed the feelings around my sudden departure from work. To my surprise, a calm came and remained with me even after my return home. The nagging sense of guilt that I had anticipated wasn't there. Like walking out of an abusive relationship, it felt like I had made the right decision, the only decision.

Kelly had also given notice at her work several weeks earlier. After the retreat she flew to Maui to join her brother and family for a couple of weeks' holiday. The family had rented out their Vancouver Island home and were taking a three-month sabbatical from their hectic life.

There was a sense of normalcy to it all. I got supporting letters from my family doctor and chiropractor to file with my medical claim with Employment Canada. The government responded quickly, informing me that my claim would be effective immediately and there would be no penalties or waiting period. I felt supported by the universe and took the time to consider my options. I needed time to heal. This would be the opportunity to begin a gentle search for a new way of earning a living.

After about one month of rest I followed up on an advertisement for a Shiatsu practitioner's course. While I knew nothing about this form of Japanese hands-on-healing, I decided to attend a complimentary session to check it out. I was intrigued by ancient eastern medicine and philosophy and I also noticed that the course offered classes in Tai Chi and bio-energetic therapy sessions. At the center, I received a powerful treatment and thought that this was something I could do.

I submitted an application, attended an interview and paid a down payment on my tuition. It seemed like an opportunity to heal as I learned. If all worked out, after a one-year course I could start my own Shiatsu practice and work with people in a healing environment.

124

In January I began my studies in Shiatsu. The limitations of my lack of physical flexibility and lower back pain immediately became apparent. Not to worry, my instructor advised, these conditions would gradually improve as the year progressed. He also offered that my weakened kidney condition controlled my chi energy base and over a period of time that these liabilities would shift and improve.

I enjoyed the classes and exchanged sessions with the other students as we practiced our techniques. People from CoDA also volunteered to let me practice on them. I had no shortage of people to work on.

I probably practiced the most on Kelly. We were spending a lot of time together, walking the sea wall and going for soup. I liked my new life and my happiness was growing daily. My lungs were improving and I was feeling more balanced and centered than I had for some time.

Toward the end of January, Kelly's former partner came to the city and attempted to reconcile with her. That was unsuccessful but had a domino effect on our relationship. Both of us realized that our feelings for each other had grown deeper than we had cared to admit. We met for lunch in a restaurant and talked it over. The feelings were mutual and we wanted to move to the next level and attempt a relationship.

There was one glitch. We had developed a solid friendship over the last year or so and had begun to develop intimacy and respect for each other. Kelly admitted that she knew more about me and had shared more about herself with me than she had done in ten years with her former partner. We were afraid to jeopardize our friendship. Our concern was that, if it didn't work out, we would lose this great friendship. We were reluctant to take the risk.

After pondering this separately and together, we decided to follow our hearts and made the commitment to enter into a relationship. Kelly had just turned thirty years old and had been in two long-term relationships. I was forty-four and had never been in a committed relationship in my life.

La la land lasted about one week and then we had our first fight. That became our pattern - push and pull, bliss and hate. We were amazed when we managed to get back together, then again when we survived another week. It was truly a miracle when the first month anniversary arrived.

This was the beginning of my relationship recovery and a defining moment in my life path. No longer could I sit back at my CoDA meetings and calmly maintain an air of recovery. Relationship recovery took on a new meaning for me. The relationship with Kelly signaled the first day of the rest of my life. The ultimate journey had begun!

Chapter Eight

Entering a Committed Relationship

Blue sky and brilliant, morning sunshine broke through the intermittent mist that skirted the ridge across the lake. A uniform luminescent dusting of new snow softly blanketed the branches of the evergreens at the higher levels while the dull, new-growth forest near the water's edge stood in stark contrast, a rooted reminder of the status quo. The call of a seagull nearby brought me back to the present as I hunched over my writing table.

I watched the intense and passionate morning sun slowly melt that fine, white layer of powder and routinely return the trees to the forest. The honeymoon hours ended as quickly as they had begun.

My fear of intimacy was rooted in understanding that I was doomed to repeat my past. Old sayings like "the sins of the father" and "like father like son" merely reinforced the belief that my life would be a replica of my childhood experience. Like the fresh snow melting away to reveal the forest's fundamental makeup, I reasoned that there was little hope for a better future for myself.

This was the reasoning that had led me to make rash pre-teen decisions that channeled the course of my adult life. It wasn't easy to change

127

those immature choices; they were cemented into the wall of my reactive childhood belief system – an inadequate foundation that undermined my efforts for decades.

The choice to enter into a relationship with Kelly was as fundamental a decision as the one I had made to enter recovery. It meant that I had to let go of the notion that I would never, ever, enter a permanent relationship or decide to marry. My childhood fear had been that I would grow up to be a kind of monster that would destroy the happiness of my prospective bride who would gradually become a sniveling wretch that cowered in hopelessness and despair. That fear meant that I would never have children. That choice played out my childhood drama of exacting a slow, absolute revenge on my parents by depriving them of the joy of knowing a grandchild.

The burden of these irrevocable decisions had weighed heavily on me for many years. Now that I decided to attempt a relationship, the negative internal voices began their familiar destructive pattern of eroding the positive commitment that I had undertaken. Within days Kelly and I experienced old feelings that had characterized our family histories. This time it wasn't our families that were serving as triggers to these episodes; it was each other. The consequence that we feared most from risking this new relationship – an inevitable breakup and the loss of our one-year friendship – seemed destined to happen. We felt powerless to stop the process of disintegration.

Neither of us was in therapy and the benefit that we derived from our CoDA meetings was not enough to fulfill our desperate need for support. We had been serving as co-sponsors for each other; now that we were romantically involved we had lost the detachment we needed to be able to hear each other objectively.

Our processing styles were also different. Kelly wanted to talk things through immediately while I needed time for the dust to settle so I could gain a sense of what the issue was about. As a consequence our relationship defaulted into fits and starts: a routine of coming together, attempting intimacy, engaging in conflict, distancing for several days, attempting resolution and then repeating the process.

We both doubted that we could or would get through it. We knew we needed help. The obvious problem was our lack of faith and trust in a higher power. We were convinced that we weren't working our programs properly and that we needed to find a greater sense of spiritual help.

My response was to begin a frantic search for external means to rectify this deficiency. I began a desperate search of new age meetings and groups, becoming a workshop junkie in hopes of finding that external fix to my problem. I no longer had the guiding hand of my previous mentor. With this lack of discernment, I was wide open to anything that came along. There were workshops by people who claimed to channel ancient spirits, others who were connected to the angelic realm and Christ consciousness, and even those who claimed to be walk-ins (an alien consciousness that has taken over a human's body). They each spoke of spiritual solutions to all problems. I trusted them and believed that my answers would be forthcoming.

Years earlier John Bradshaw had warned about getting lost in higher consciousness. I didn't see how this could apply to my situation and continued my desperate odyssey. The group that became a focus of my attention had a copper meditation chamber called a stargate whose design had been channeled by a bodywork therapist. The purpose of the stargate was to anchor energy and promote healing on a global level. There were approximately fifty of these stargates around the world. I enrolled in the group's practitioner's workshop. The husband and wife team that led this spiritual group originated in Europe and had lived in Vancouver, Hawaii and Colorado. Because of their travels, they had ties around the world.

Not only did I participate but also like several other local people, I purchased a stargate of my own. My vision was to practice Shiatsu when I completed that yearlong course. Then I could help other people release their issues through a combination of body and energy work, the stargate being a significant tool for my practice. I had learned from receiving polarity therapy and bio-energetic therapy that people store old memories and trauma at a cellular level. These internalized issues manifest as disease if they are not dealt with. Certain types of trauma and stress are stored in specific areas of the body-neck, back and pelvis. I planned to fine-tune this knowledge to become a successful practitioner.

Another significant direction came from one of the stargate practitioners from Hawaii. She said that the stargate enhanced the individual's process of self-actualization and she dared me to take ownership of my own process. The challenge was to become all that we could be. I was intrigued and took up the challenge.

Kelly did not participate in this stargate workshop; she gave me distanced support to follow my path. The practitioner's course lasted for one week encompassing a wide range of spiritual practices from releasing limiting beliefs and becoming open to new forms of non-linear thinking, to channeling and energetic healing.

After completing the course, I found myself no farther ahead in the search for the spiritual assistance that I had hoped for. Although I now had a stargate in my apartment, besides some sort of spiritual connectedness there was no apparent benefit from this copper device the size of a three-man tent. True, it was the outward manifestation of an inner process. However, the inter-dimensional gateway provided no immediate solution to my intimacy problems with my new partner.

In fact, I was beginning to develop more relationship problems in my Shiatsu practitioner's course. One of the aspects of the program was to be part of an ongoing therapy group with a bio-energetic practitioner. I felt this practitioner was unsafe, confrontational and not real. I withdrew from the group therapy portion of the program and that placed me on the outside from the balance of the Shiatsu students. To make things worse, I had difficulty with the Tai Chi study and couldn't keep up with the others. If this wasn't enough, our anatomy professor was incompetent and everyone in the class wanted him to be replaced. Things slowly got worse.

My self-esteem was taking direct hits from all of these perceived failures to fit in. My recent track record now included an unsuccessful experience with the bookstore owners, conflict in twelve step groups, major setbacks in therapy, ostracism in the workplace and my first post-recovery friendship had ended badly. Here I was again with my first real relationship in jeopardy and it didn't appear that my practitioner's course was going to work out for me. What was the matter with me? Why weren't things working out?

The old belief system clicked into gear and the negative self-talk surfaced. A Course in Miracles referred to that form of self-talk as the ego. The Course said that the ego was our greatest enemy that was always ready to preach catastrophe and fear, and was actually conspiring to kill us. My old belief system told me that things never worked out for me; there was no sense in hoping for something different. Everything always ended badly for me.

The good thing about being in a push-pull relationship means that there are times together and when you can offer each other support. Although my tendency was to reject everything when hope seemed to wane, Kelly consistently maintained a belief in her higher power. Her faith was an inspiration for me. Her strength and conviction pulled me through the blackest periods.

There were also other sources of hope. I was still involved in the planning process for the national Canadian CoDA convention. One of the perks was that Kelly and I had the opportunity to share some special time with Ken and Mary R., the founders of CoDA. They were coming to Vancouver to participate in our first national service conference and they were to be our keynote speakers at the convention. They were registered therapists in Arizona and probably had as much knowledge about relationship issues as anyone in the country. They were married and had gone through the same initial problems that we were encountering, so we hoped that they could shed some light on our situation.

While we were searching for housing for the CoDA convention, we found a new bed and breakfast in North Vancouver that was advertised in *Shared Vision,* a local holistic publication. We rented the entire home for the CoDA founders and the provincial delegates from across Canada.

Our first Canadian conference lasted for two days, and then we attended our first Canadian convention, which took place at Trinity College, a small campus we rented in the Fraser Valley. The convention was well-attended and, on the surface, it appeared to be a huge success. This is when I began to learn about the different levels that occur simultaneously as events play out.

Each convention took on a life of its own. This was a lesson in acknowledging there were things we could not control. No matter how we fine-tuned our agenda and program with choices of speakers and workshops, entertainment and meals, complications came up. The people who attended had a unique combined energy. Ultimately the entire weekend took on the personality of that group consciousness. Prior to my stargate experience, I was so invested in linear thinking that I couldn't appreciate the multidimensional aspects of such a situation.

For the previous year, unbeknownst to the general membership of CoDA, nasty rumors circulated about underhanded dealings among some of the delegates to the world service conference. Cruel words were spoken including personal attacks on the founders and the trustees. These plays for power and control were the outgrowth of unhealthy relationships. Unfortunately, petty politics escalated to court cases. While the trustees became the targets of aggression and verbal abuse, the founders discovered themselves in the unenviable position of bull's eyes. They attempted to handle the attacks with as much grace as possible and concealed the sordid details from the convention participants by maintaining their grounding, honor and balance.

For the one hundred and fifty attendees at the convention, little of these unfortunate circumstances came to light. They attended the workshops, enjoyed the special events and entertainment and returned home happier, healthier and full of hope for continued growth in recovery.

What did I get from all this? I was reminded of what I had learned years earlier in therapy. The mark of a person's recovery is his or her ability to respond rather than react in a given situation. Ken and Mary had shown their recovery by responding well under difficult circumstances. They had talked about the issues and they had honestly expressed their genuine feelings. This was what I needed to see in order to continue on my road to recovery. I had been doing the work. My biggest problem was my expectation that, because I had been in recovery and in therapy, things wouldn't affect me any longer. Wrong! Once again, I needed to make the association between reacting and responding.

But why were so many things in my own life not working out?

I was beginning to see that relationships are difficult for most if not all people. Some never attempt to achieve intimacy because the pain and risk are too overwhelming. They distract themselves. They engage in addictive and compulsive behaviors. They hide behind their defense tactics: discounting, minimizing and denying any semblance of problems.

Recovery isn't for wimps and neither is doing the work in relationships. What Kelly and I found was that unresolved issues from our childhood kept coming up and so did the feelings. We recommitted to what we had learned. One part of this process was to own our feelings by using "I" statements. That meant saying "I feel," "I want," "I need," rather than "you" or "they" statements. Further, we resolved to try to not take on the other person's stuff and not to take things personally.

And if we weren't struggling with everyday issues, our attempts at sexual intimacy were emotional dynamite. Another level, another set of issues. While we both enjoyed sex, we both had performance anxiety over it. As a consequence, we each had a difficult time staying present during a sexual experience. One or the other, or both of us would split into our head and the whole process would come to a frustrating end. We learned to talk about what was making us split and slowly we got to the point where we could have mutually satisfying experiences. We had to accept that it was all a process and that by doing the work we would see slow, steady improvement.

As September approached again, it was time for me to attend the CoDA service conference in Phoenix. I had made arrangements with one of the original CoDA members to do several days of sightseeing together prior to the actual conference. She was heavily involved in native spirituality, leading and participating in healing circles. She had organized one in Vancouver when she had been the keynote speaker at our provincial convention one year prior.

We spent time in Sedona exploring energy vortices and medicine wheels in several power spots. Then we visited ruins and cave dwellings from several different native cultures. After touring for several days, a remarkable event occurred for me. It was a follow-on from my vision quest of the year before.

Between Phoenix and Tucson, we visited a native center that included an art gallery as well as four distinct village replicas. They showed how things functioned hundreds of years ago. The exhibit complex was fenced with a thick adobe wall where a native artist was applying murals. In the midst of his painting was a drawing of a man standing and holding a huge round plaque over his head. The plaque had an old native design of a man standing outside a maze.

The image was identical to the form of the shadows I had seen in the southern landscape every evening while on my vision quest. The man and the maze were further details revealed by this mural. When we asked the artist about the significance of his painting, he told us that the only way for man to escape the puzzle of his personal maze was through the process of acceptance. Each man needs to accomplish that acceptance in his own way.

Seeing my own vision in the mural gave me goose bumps. The message was there for me; now to apply it to my own journey. I needed to trust that over time the exact meaning would be revealed in a personally profound way.

The combination of the vision quest and the revelation in the Arizona desert had a powerful effect on me. To some degree I felt more connected and assured of myself. I was coming home to myself – returning to a place of personal power in relation to my world. This was a timely shift for me because things were about to get completely out of control at the service conference.

When the conference came together, all the back room deals and splinter group alliances that had been formed via telephone, email and correspondence over the past several years finally surfaced. The conference was more like a mutiny than anything else.

If I ever had the idea that people at the international level of service reflected a congruent level of recovery and demonstrated practiced recovery principles, that notion was forever shattered at this conference. There were two levels of delegates present – those committed to service work who were eager to participate in the conference and those who were politically sophisticated and subversive. This second group was like a gang of angry teenagers: aggressive, abusive and full of attitude. They had no intention of allowing the conference to proceed.

The dissension deteriorated so quickly that the conference had to be stopped for the issues to be addressed. We began with a group meditation asking for unity, clarity and healing. That was followed by microphone time where each delegate was allowed three minutes at the mike. There was to be no heckling, cross talk or interruptions. Each person was to share his or her truth.

After about one third of the delegates (about thirty or so people) had been heard, there was no need to continue. Everything that needed to be aired had been put into the room. Everyone had been heard. This was a remarkable demonstration of the recovery process and there was a significant shift in energy.

The conference resumed and it seemed that everything was moving forward again. Then, one group had begun a filibuster that threatened to completely undermine the conference. What a waste of time and money.

Through organizing and attending various conferences, we had all learned a lot about parliamentary procedure. This time, I addressed the issue at a window of parliamentary opportunity. A vote was called and the dissenting committee was directed to discontinue its filibuster. The conference was back on track.

It felt good to be of service in this manner. The empowerment of that moment stayed with me for the duration of the conference. When it came time for my report on the upcoming world convention, I presented a strong update on our committee's work and then fielded a barrage of questions. Because I worked closely with all the committees on a continual basis, I had no problem in handling the interrogation. This further success bolstered my confidence and, on a deeper level, added to my building esteem and recovery in conflict resolution.

The last piece of business at the conference was the election of trustees. This year my bid was enthusiastically received, culminating in my being voted to the position of trustee for world service. This newly elected trustee to the Board of Directors of an International Corporation (CoDA) was the same person who had been declared chronically angry, emotionally unstable and unlikely to be employable again in his life. Finally I was winning battles, doing business and gaining recognition for my hard work and dedication to service. The rewards were beyond my wildest imagination.

One trustee whose term of service had expired the previous year had been told earlier in life that she would never walk again. She had proved them wrong. Now here I was, in my way, demonstrating that I could be an effective, contributing part of society. This was a big day for me and also for the other Canadian delegates. Besides my personal triumph, I had become the first person from outside the United States to be elected to this level of service.

This series of events showed me the importance of maintaining a strong program of recovery and a personal commitment to a higher power. I was beginning to understand that the real work was internal. There was no need to maintain a constant, desperate search for an external solution to my problems. I needed to learn to go within myself to connect in a more personal way with my own inner guidance. This was a simple concept – one that I had heard repeatedly yet never properly assimilated.

Late that fall another significant milestone occurred in my life. Kelly accompanied me to my parent's house for Thanksgiving. My usual trips home had a similar pattern: five or ten minutes talking to my parents, then my father retreated into his book or the TV while my mother went into the kitchen to get supper ready. Each time, after supper I usually left as quickly as possible. Kelly had met my parents that summer. Now, at the holiday meal with Kelly in the picture, the dynamic changed. It was not so much different with my father; the change was more significant with my mother. Kelly and I joined her in the kitchen and actually had a conversation. Then after supper, the three of us played cards. We laughed and chatted and had fun! This was definitely new for our household.

Including Kelly was the beginning of a new relationship with my family. My parents loved Kelly and were happy with my choice. The unhealthy decisions I had made in childhood were fast dissolving. Gradually I allowed my parents to receive some degree of happiness from my misguided life. There was a piece in me that was softening and it felt good. For too long I had been hardened to the razor's edge of revenge and bitterness.

This softening within me did not extend to my Shiatsu school situation. I had passed the point of caring about, or even showing interest in, completing the training program. With only one month to go before the final exam and practicum, I withdrew from the course. I attempted to do it in a positive, non-blaming way. But I must have put my foot in my mouth because my withdrawal wasn't well received. I had no intention of completing the required studies nor did I expect to pay the balance of my tuition. I spoke my truth, presented my case and walked away.

On one level I was sad. Here was another hopeful start that had ended in a missed opportunity. I worked hard not to internalize the message that I was a failure. Instead, I reviewed the facts as I saw them: a combination of inadequate instruction and a therapist I could not work with. I had paid a significant portion of my fees but decided that paying for everything would further enable a weak system to continue. Deciding to say no demonstrated my personal power over my environment.

The year was coming to an end. Seeking another route back into the system, I registered for another job reentry program in the new year. This time the program was downtown through an agency that specialized in testing, preparing resumes and headhunting for major corporations.

Within my recovery bubble, I saw myself as successful and hoped that my accomplishments and personal growth would readily transpose to the mainstream world. The testing revealed that my emotional profile was overly sensitive and presented as a possible liability. The agency advised that if I wanted to earn money in the corporate world that I should concentrate on entering the field of sales. I had been down that road in my early twenties and it was not one that I wished to repeat.

The alternative suggestion was that I re-enter my former occupation in turf management in a less responsible capacity. Although I was reluctant to do this, fear and time lines prompted me to disregard my inner sense of rightness. I applied to an advertisement in the newspaper and was immediately hired onto the crew of one of the city's older private golf courses.

From the first day I knew that it was a mistake, yet I persisted out of desperation. It's difficult to begin a new job. There is so much to learn and there is the pressure to fit in and become part of the team. When the position is entry level and the average age of the crew is twenty years or more younger than the new person, the pressure is magnified. When I added my higher educational background and management experience to the package, I was again an outsider. The odds were exponentially stacked against me but I wanted to work.

As I got to know people, they asked questions and became aware of my background. It became generally known that I had worked at some established courses. My former positions both as assistant superintendent and superintendent surfaced as did my efforts at recovery from alcohol and drugs. All the way, I was the odd man out. Conflict emerged, particularly with one employee who also had a personal history of abuse and chemical dependency. Although it had not been my intent to get enmeshed in his life, we shared conversations as we worked and I exceeded appropriate boundaries. It was a lesson for me in discernment but the damage was done. I had allowed too much of my personal life to enter into the work environment. My alienation from my former job at the parks department was repeated.

My life seemed out of control. I was struggling and failing, attempting to force myself to succeed at something I had abandoned years earlier. I had no desire to work on a golf course again but I had let myself be talked into it by the employment agency. This set-up for failure caused me to feel terrible about myself and to further doubt my ability to succeed in the work place. I was definitely not following my path.

My relationship with Kelly was going well and we were talking about moving in together. Actually, she was talking about it and I was getting cold feet. I wasn't ready to make the move; the timing didn't seem right. My sense of stability was shaken by my work situation. I feared if I lost my job, I would not be able to hold up my end financially.

It was at this point that the world CoDA convention took place. Apart from my role as convention chairperson, I also had the privilege of serving as emcee. Everything flowed because I was doing what I loved. The busyness and pace of the weekend were exhilarating. In this aspect of my life everything flowed effortlessly. Why couldn't my life and work be like this in the real world?

I felt safe in the context of the CoDA convention and my attention to detail and sense of logistics served me well. I delegated responsibilities and handled the role of emcee with warmth and flexibility.

People attended from other countries and continents. Although we numbered under two hundred people, we came together and shared our experience, strength and hope. We worked hard, cried, played and laughed. We brought with us a sense of belonging and commitment to growth and personal accountability. We felt important and each of us returned home with the conviction that the ripple effect would touch others we came in contact with.

Riding on the high of the convention's success, I consented to move in with Kelly. After several weeks of looking for a suitable place, we rented the upper floor of a house where we had a kitchen, dining room, living room and three bedrooms. We each wanted personal space in case things weren't working too well. This home with a large yard and mature vegetation was in a lovely, older middle-class neighborhood. The cost was equal to the sum of the two apartments we had been renting so it seemed to be within our means.

We booked a moving truck for the next weekend, confident that we could handle the job ourselves. We had no idea how much work it would entail. After working Friday evening and all day Saturday we had managed to pack and move the contents of Kelly's apartment. We were exhausted. There was no way we could finish the job by ourselves and we didn't feel comfortable asking people to help us because, after all, moving was not a fun thing.

Inspiration struck. We drove to McDonalds where we planned to hire some teenagers to help us. Our eccentric attempt bore fruit and we found someone who was willing to help us out. Together we got the job completed and the moving van returned.

My furniture was completely different, in style, color and size from Kelly's but somehow it didn't matter. We made it work and all our guests remarked on how comfy and warm our place felt. It must have been the energy because everything worked out. One of the spare bedrooms became our storage and ironing room, while the other became a telephone room. We had space, warmth and all the hope that new couples share.

Yet we both were having problems at work. Kelly had taken a part-time job as a childcare worker. Within a matter of months she had been asked to work full-time, then act as the assistant supervisor and then had been made supervisor of an eight-bed group home. The kids in the home were out of control and there were major staffing problems.

It hurt me to watch her get up in the morning and sit on the edge of the bed and burst into tears. She never wanted to go to work. It was constant chaos and she was never heard or supported by upper management.

Things weren't going any better for me at the golf course. I didn't like my superintendent. His assistant was incompetent and I hated the conflict and alienation I was experiencing from my co-workers. There was no way that I could be able to stand the one or two years working my way back up to management, at least not at this golf course.

I began to doubt myself again. All my golf course management experience had been in Alberta, a prairie province where desiccation and wind had been the constant factors. Now I was in a different environment facing new conditions – excessive moisture and related turf diseases. I just didn't have the energy to put into re-learning and re-thinking this line of work. But I didn't know what else I could do or where I should go from here.

Just when everything seemed like it was about to fall apart, I received a phone call from one of the more affluent municipalities near home where I had submitted a resume. They needed one person to complete a two-man staff at a public pitch and putt golf course. I successfully interviewed, quit my golf course job and began my new duties within two days. The pay was considerably higher and the conditions and benefits were superior.

I had never worked at a pitch and putt and, to tell the truth, had never considered it to even qualify as a golf course. I had extensive experience at the private course level and had a diploma from a recognized institution. My new supervisor had neither. We had completely different approaches to our work. Tension and differences of opinion emerged on the first day. Once again, I found myself in a position that wasn't really what I wanted.

My problem was that I didn't know what I did want. I had no sense of direction and little motivation. I felt powerless and frustrated in the work place. Within two months, I was fired from the new position. I didn't even survive the probation period.

That experience left me feeling deflated and dejected. I needed to work because, for the first time in my life, I shared the responsibility of managing a home. I panicked. Over several days I compiled a list of the golf courses with the names of the superintendents in the entire Lower Mainland. Then I spent one week traveling to each of the courses where I personally delivered the resume and cover letter to each superintendent. The grand result was that no one wanted to hire me.

I was frantic. I didn't know what to do. In spite of her own problems at work, Kelly supported me the best she could under adverse conditions. I now knew for sure that I'd had enough of golf courses. If that hadn't been entirely obvious to me, the lack of response from my resume blitz demonstrated that there was no interest on their part. The universe thought so too.

So like a kid who doesn't know where to turn or what to do, I prayed. Maybe I should say I groveled and begged my higher power to help me. To my amazement, a new concept began to form in my head: why not work in some aspect of recovery - helping people who wanted help? The seedling thought germinated and I quickly wrote a resume based on my recovery experience.

One of the concepts that I had learned through the job re-entry programs was the technique of the informational interview. A woman I knew from my involvement with helping professions was the executive director of a native tribe social agency. In fact, she was the director of the agency that employed Kelly. I made an appointment for an informational interview with her in the hope that she could direct me to people who might be interested in talking with me about possible employment. To my surprise, she offered me a job as a childcare worker in a different area from Kelly. The woman was supportive of my service work and consented to hire me upon my return from the annual service conference in Phoenix in September.

I had mixed emotions about attending the service conference in Phoenix. My role as a trustee for world service placed me in a different capacity than I had previously enjoyed as a delegate. There had been no cohesion with the new board of trustees. The new chairperson, the only holdover from the previous executive, had resigned. There had been no chance to work together to achieve resolution of the many demands that confronted the board. Instead there had been secret alliances and power struggles.

I was outside of the new loop. Although I definitely had strong opinions about the apparent mismanagement of the issues at hand, no one was hearing my point of view. I was appalled by the callous manner in which this board handled its full-time employees. I was enraged by the petty politics that surrounded the writing, editing and publishing of the CoDA book. I was dismayed by the change in conference structure. There seemed to be prearranged alliances formed before every conference call and every meeting. I lost confidence in the board and found it difficult to continue.

Still there was cause for celebration of the board's appreciation of my contribution. I was happy to be chairing the convention committee. We had done well in Vancouver and had presented the conference and the new committee chairpersons with seed money to begin work on the next world convention.

It felt like my time as a trustee was coming to an end. The people at my last job re-entry program had been amazed by the level of responsibility I had undertaken as a volunteer in service work. It was their opinion that this level of responsibility should be served by full-time, paid board members. They had been wrong about my ability to succeed back on the golf course. Were they wrong here?

I had major decisions to make. With a new job to begin upon my return to Vancouver, it was important for me to be clear on what I wanted. I didn't want to repeat my recent track record of unhappy employment. I needed to achieve success and happiness from my employment comparable to what I had gained from my efforts in service work. If I could excel in one area, why couldn't I in the other?

After soul searching, Kelly and I had decided on our priorities, putting our health first, relationship second, children and family third and career a distant fourth. I had always believed that career was supposed to be number one. Clearly, my life was about to change and my belief systems were to be expanded.

PART THREE

LEARNING TO TRUST

Chapter Nine

Work and Personal Needs

The early morning sun warmed the still air that lazily covered the glassy lake, nudging it into motion. The resulting ripples refracted the light making the valley of water shimmer like a sequined shawl. The early frost had long since melted and the saturated wooden planks on the aging sundeck exhaled moisture, indicating that they would be dry by late afternoon. It promised to be a spectacular spring-like day, although February struggled to play out its monotonous hand.

Away in Salt Lake City, the winter Olympics had celebrated closing ceremonies and the participants were heading home, proud ambassadors, bearing good will and international cooperation. I had vicariously experienced the games in my usual manner, quietly blubbering in the privacy of my living room, sharing tears equally for winners, less fortunate participants and also-rans.

Looking again at the saturated boards on the sun deck, I'm sure that a cosmic process of osmosis has transferred my tears to them and transformed the deck into a podium of sorts.

Kelly simply smiles and tells me that if there was an Olympics for recovery that I'd surely win a gold. That's one of the nice things about being in a relationship, about being married – the continuous level of support makes it all worthwhile.

That support wasn't a given in the relationship; it had to be earned and nurtured as we grew in intimacy. Many times when we needed it, it wasn't available to us. Emotional issues, power struggles and periods of overwhelming stress robbed us, time and again, of being present for each other. We had to do the work, risk and bring all our stuff to light.

In the beginning, all we knew how to do was build brick walls between us. Sharing, and allowing each other to voice all of our concerns, slowly developed trust and safety at progressively deeper levels. That led to hearing each other out. We finally got to a point where we could extend this support to, and depend on, each other.

Some people say that they never quarrel in their relationship and others insist that it isn't spiritual to get angry. We disagree. We believe that to deny the intensity and feelings behind issues is unhealthy. These internalized emotions manifest disease and eventually will lead to sickness. The challenge is to express feelings appropriately and honor your partner at the same time.

Too often we failed to do that, wanting to inflict wounds on the other that were equal to our own pain. That kind of psychic attack is deeply hurtful and can lead to lack of trust and relationship breakdown. Fair fighting and boundary setting are essential recovery tools that need to be honed and consistently applied.

This was the work that I was faced with, that fall, when I began my career as a childcare worker. I had never intended to work with kids; I didn't believe they were ready to do any work on themselves. I much preferred working with adults who had hit a personal bottoming out. That sense of having nothing more to lose motivated and committed them to instituting change in their lives. To tell the truth, I was hesitant and nervous to be around children. I had not really enjoyed my stints as a substitute schoolteacher and I didn't particularly like teenage attitudes and behavior.

One further hurdle that I needed to clear before I could begin my new position was to look at my prejudices and race specific issues. I had never considered myself a racist. In fact, I had maintained that every culture had nice people and those whose character and behavior were less than desirable. So I felt that it wasn't a race thing but was rather an individual assessment. Either I liked people and we got along or I didn't care for them and gave them space. It had nothing to with race.

I was going to work for a First Nations agency. Until now, I had never been in a position where I had close personal dealings with First Nations people on a daily basis. In school I'd had native classmates and had social exchanges with native individuals. That had gone okay. In my early recovery I had befriended a native woman and had enjoyed the time I spent with her and her young children. She had given me my first book on native spirituality. Through my spiritual search I had attended healing circles, sweat lodges, pow wows and even done a personal vision quest.

The underlying nervousness I harbored about working closely among First Nations people had more to do with whether or not I would be accepted. This fear-based thinking was in line with my personal history. I had always feared groups, French-speaking people, Catholic people and people of higher socio-economic profiles who were confident, successful or aggressive.

I talked this over with my new supervisor who was native, and he helped me deal with my fear in several ways. First, he showed me a study that had brought several myths to light. One myth the study debunked was that only native people could successfully raise native children. We processed this information and achieved the higher ground that love and consistently healthy behavior were far more important than ethnic background. Secondly, talking about prejudice and racist feelings helped relieve the pressure.

He admitted that many adult natives disliked white people because of historical atrocities that continued to the present day. We acknowledged that these issues would come up. My task was not to take them personally but to consider the source; it would always be about the person who was projecting the anger. The best that I could do was to set boundaries, make space and not take it on.

The final piece of orientation was the most profound. We explored the scope of the job and the tribal agency's expectations. Like all social agencies, this one dealt with kids that had been badly abused, some sexually, some physically, some emotionally. There were also those who had attention deficit disorder and those who were symptomatic of fetal alcohol syndrome. My job was not to fix any of these kids, but rather to give them special time and offer myself as a healthy role model.

For the first time in my working life, I was being recognized for my accomplishments. The agency thought that my recovery and personal

147

health combined with relevant experiential and educational background was enough to trust me with their children. In short, I got to be the good guy. It was my turn.

I pondered that this work had more or less found me; it was the result of asking my higher power for help. I had surrendered to a process over which I had no control and had merely followed through on accessing a new job market. I had been open to this new direction and was happy for the opportunity to put my recovery skills and beliefs to work.

Along the way I had made a decision to view my recovery path as my life journey. I was in my tenth year of recovery and, unlike my reckless years in addiction, I now wanted my life to mean something. I wanted the world to be a better place because of things I did along the way. I had no sense of where this job would take me or even if I would be any good at it. I had been guided to it and I had the willingness to play out the hand I had been dealt.

My work began with one teen. Eventually my caseload was increased to include preteens as well. I treated all the kids the same – the way I like to be treated myself – with dignity, respect and honesty. It worked. Not only did I begin to develop relationships with the kids but also I made meaningful connections with them. As a result, I could successfully set limits and boundaries. I learned and applied basic parenting skills using a consistent approach. In short, I said what I meant and meant what I said.

My relationship with Kelly was slowly developing, however we continued to fight, cut off and distance. It became common for us to go one or two or even several days without talking. We both hated this silent treatment and were grateful when we were able to affect resolution and get back on track. Our work was demanding and brought out the intensity in us. Kelly had several girlfriends that she could continually process her stuff with. I realized that it would be nice if I had someone else to talk with as well. I had never been successful in forming co-sponsor relationships or friendships with men in the program. I had made several attempts but it never flowed and always felt forced.

I decided to start a men's CoDA group and see how that would work for me. One night per week for several months, I met with a group of guys out of our Saturday morning CoDA home group. It didn't work for me. I never felt safe and there was always pressure on me to make it work.

I had seen problems like this before in special interest groups. At one point, a specialized group of social workers and therapists had been formed in the city to give them a space where they didn't risk their clients showing up. Several of the professionals in that group were friends of mine and they had shared their frustrations about the meetings. There was an underlying worry of judgment by their professional colleagues so they were unable to be vulnerable or to appear not to have it together. All these people were getting together and no one was being real. The meeting flopped.

At the men's meeting, something similar was happening. It took me awhile to get the sense of the problem. Almost all of the men were in other twelve step programs and had come to CoDA because they had problems in sustaining relationships. Over time I realized that they had a hidden agenda. Each wanted to find a relationship for himself. There was nothing wrong with this – in fact a meeting is probably the best place for a recovering person to find a partner. What wasn't okay, though, was to be hitting on women at the meeting. Over a period of time, the men's agenda became blatantly obvious. Women complained that the meeting was no longer safe.

We addressed the issue at the meeting but meetings and people can't be controlled. Soon, a pervasive tension transmitted back to my home group and the attendance declined. I attempted to address this problem with a core group of the guys during lunch after one of our meetings. They weren't interested in talking about it; they were more interested in talking sports and discussing the physical attributes of female group members who had attended the meeting.

They weren't getting it. You can't come across as a vulnerable, supportive person in the meeting and then revert to "tits and ass" as soon as you leave the church. It isn't congruent and it's obvious. I told them so and refused to sit with them. There was no love lost between us.

My feeling of being estranged from the men in the groups was becoming a recurring issue. Someone suggested that these dynamics would keep coming up until I had completed the unfinished business around my father. The dissension was carried into the men's group and my role as scapegoat resurfaced.

The straw that broke the camel's back came in the men's group. There were half dozen men in the group who weren't in recovery from substance abuse; instead of going for coffee after the meetings, they began to go to a nearby pub to continue the discussion over drinks. This hit me hard. One of the essential pieces in any twelve-step meeting is anonymity. Every meeting closed with the statement "whatever is said here, stays here." It was inappropriate to extend these discussions into a public venue, especially where alcohol was being consumed. Alcohol and boundaries are mutually exclusive. For me, confidentiality and safety could no longer be associated with either the men's group or the home group.

I had to decide if I could continue to attend. This wasn't a decision to take lightly. My twelve-step program was my lifeline and it was unraveling in front of me.

To make matters worse, I continued to doubt my participation in CoDA international service work. I was receiving no response from key committee heads in the United States. Politics once again overrode the recovery basis of the organization on several levels. I had seen the viciousness of the past several years prey upon board members. I decided that I would not endure that level of abuse.

Another complication was that some details concerning CoDA's past history were coming to light. I learned that several years earlier CoDA had threatened legal action against the minister in the eastern states whose authority encompassed the church where we had our first Canadian meeting. There had been an out-of-court settlement but as a result the church in Vancouver had been directed to cancel its CoDA meeting. I also learned that several recovery speakers had allied to do a personal recovery intervention on a prominent recovery author, speaker and guru.

Stability was lacking on every level. I experienced an extreme escalation of stress. My initial response due to my overdeveloped sense of responsibility was to attempt to fix as much of the situation as possible but something held me back. In order for a therapeutic process to be successful there has to be an honest, committed effort from all partners. I saw that this was not the case with my home groups, with the committee members or the trustees on the board. There was chaos and levels of denial.

With the likelihood that change could not be effected, I decided that the healthy response was to focus on self-care. This caused some initial feelings of guilt and I underwent a round of negative thoughts labeling myself a quitter and a loser.

Quieting my negative self-talk, I protected myself by resigning. In short order, I stopped attending my local meetings and stepped down from my position on the CoDA board. It was time to let go of the extra stressors in my life and focus on what was important. The first thing was my health. I needed to recommit to my personal holistic wellness plan and get things in order. I needed to concentrate on making my relationship with Kelly successful. I had to trust that I had learned enough of the basic skills to make that probable. I needed to focus energy into my new career and maintain a centered, grounded place of balance from which I could operate.

It was time to let go of the externals and begin the process of trusting my higher power on a deeper level, a more personal level where I could better establish a relationship and begin to rely more on my inner wisdom. This decision to care for myself was liberating. Suddenly I had more time and energy to invest in my relationship.

Things were still difficult for Kelly at work. She was undergoing maximum stress dealing with her staff and the inconsistencies within the system.

In spite of her work problems, we had more time to spend together and began to do things together that we enjoyed. On weekends we often crossed into the U.S. and went secondhand shopping in Bellingham, Lynden and Mt. Vernon. We loved a scavenger hunt and consistently found name brand treasures for next to nothing. We developed a string of favorite restaurants and places to stay. Finally we were having fun.

At the same time, we were slowly forming a relationship with my parents. For the first time in years I could be comfortable around my father for more than just a few minutes. That had limits though, so we focused our attention on my mother. We enjoyed traveling out to their house for a visit, for the good home-cooked meals mom prepared and for our shared passion of playing cards.

One of the issues that led Kelly to recovery was her gambling. She had been a high stakes card player and member of several poker clubs. I had played some poker in my past and we both enjoyed the feeling of control and sense of management that playing cards gives, more than the competition or actual money exchange. We thrived on the social aspect of cards.

My mother invited a couple of her friends and we made regular evenings of cards on our visits to my parents' home. We played for pennies, our enjoyment coming from the hilarity that inevitably arose. My father did not take part. He would join us for dinner but always withdrew to his book or television program.

We also played cards when we went to Vancouver Island to visit Kelly's large family. Having arrived in BC from Manitoba in the 1950's, first Kelly's dad and a couple of brothers came, then gradually more and more of the family joined them.

She had a bigger family than I had expected.

My grandfather (the surgeon) had been one of eleven kids. From an even bigger family, Kelly's dad was one of eighteen. Like my mother's background of split family, Kelly's dad's clan had an even more complicated makeup. On one occasion Kelly's grandfather explained the whole thing to me. I'm not particularly good at remembering the complicated connections, but he maintained in the end that he was his own grandpa! That was the sense of the large family – lots of laughs – and they loved to play cards. Kelly's dad was, at least in his own mind, one of the best card players in his family. He was highly entertaining and liked to play fast, in fact, he usually played everyone else's hand as well as his own. Needless to say, we played cards at her extended family's homes as well. Kelly's brother and sister and their families also played cards.

Cards and a love of music seemed to be the bond cementing the family. Many of Kelly's aunts, uncles and cousins played guitar and some had sung in choirs. Kelly's dad had his own band for a while.

The passion of Kelly's family was sports. Like many Canadian hockey families, their loyalties were divided between the Toronto Maple Leafs and the Montreal Canadiens. But times change, and some of the family members were intensely into statistics and hockey pools.

It seemed like a natural family blend for me. I loved music, sports and cards. But I was overwhelmed by the size of the family and could never keep track of who was who. Because I was new, they all knew my name. It got to the point where I was afraid to go downtown, worried that I might offend someone because I didn't remember them. Then I realized that even family members couldn't keep track of everyone.

My sense of being overwhelmed was complicated by an unexpected factor. My recovery stuff got in the way of bonding with Kelly's family. It wasn't my abstention from alcohol that interfered, it was my emotional sensitivity and inability to set healthy boundaries in situations similar to those that had been abusive earlier in my life.

Part of the dynamics of a family this size is the social banter that occurs between family members. It is a way in which many people bond.

152

To me, the banter seemed more like low-level conflict, a form of passive aggressive violence. Throughout my life I had witnessed people making snide and catty comments at other people's expense. I didn't like it. More recently I had been involved in the dissension between the men and women in my home recovery group. Having regarded that conflict as unhealthy, I had my guard up.

At Christmas with Kelly's family, when the banter was innocently directed at me I responded in a prickly manner. The family member who had been anticipating a good-natured comeback was shocked. To make it worse, I repeated the faux pas during a card game. During one of those prolonged silences that followed I realized that I had committed the ultimate social blunder. I had offended my hostess and shamed her in front of her family. The damage had been done and we returned home to the mainland.

Winter gave way to spring as we continued to visit my parents, play cards and develop a relationship. On one weekend at my parent's house we were looking in the used car ads and discovered a vehicle to check out on the way home. Kelly had visualized herself driving a white Miata and we had been searching for several months. When we approached the seller's home, Kelly saw the gleaming, waxed sports car in the driveway. She gasped, "This is the one!"

The car had been in an accident and had been rebuilt. This had no bearing on Kelly's decision. She loved the car and the next day we started the process of obtaining a bank loan. Because of having been re-built, the car was selling for about five thousand less than the other ones we had test-driven. There was another interested buyer so our time frame was restricted. Within two days, Kelly's car loan was rejected by five major banks. Still, she remained determined. She had begun the imaging process when she was unemployed and had remained focused on her vision. She intuited that this was to be her car. She had created it and she wasn't going to give up.

Within a few minutes of closing time, we approached a newer bank. They consented to lend us the money based on both our incomes. This was the first time that we had combined our assets and we were pleased to qualify. The car was hers!

The Miata fit Kelly's five foot one frame perfectly. We were in sports car heaven. Top up or top down, we had a great time. It was early spring but we wore our ski jackets and cranked up the heater with the top down. We didn't care. Somehow the hurtful events of Christmas blew away in the wind. We now focused on our everyday lives.

My work was going well and I got a sense of personal satisfaction from my efforts. Things were still chaotic for Kelly and she wasn't happy with her position. Then, the Canadian government cut back transfer payments, which meant that provincial budgets would be slashed. That affected my job security. Our agency was forced to cut staff and the first to go would be the childcare workers. We were to be cut back from approximately twenty workers to two. They would keep one male and one female.

My immediate reaction was panic. I visualized catastrophe and completely lost myself in fear. I prayed to my higher power. Slowly people came forward in support of me – Kelly, my supervisor, several of the social workers, teachers and management from schools, school board support people, psychologists and art therapists. The number of people and the kind feedback was touching and empowering. Slowly, I got the notion that I had a chance at being the one male worker retained. I was better educated and trained, older and more professional than the other child-care workers. Most important, I connected with the kids and they trusted me.

Remembering one of the first days that I had been in one of the elementary schools, a small group of kids had rushed to greet and surround a popular visiting psychologist. I had secretly said that was what I wanted for myself. Well, it had come true. The new principal at that same school had watched me with her students and she had labeled me a hot commodity. The kids paid me the same testament as they had to that therapist.

Interviews were conducted and the final announcement was posted. I was relieved to learn that I was the male care worker retained, promoted and placed on a full-time salary with extended benefits.

Financial security had always been a key issue for me. My childhood poverty and low self-esteem had created a disproportionate need for security and comfort. Now the tension factor was reduced. Kelly and I were handling our life and relationship better than we had previously. There were still the intense emotional encounters, name-calling and silent periods of distancing but they were fewer and farther between.

As summer came, we got three weeks off for our first holiday together. We decided to explore the southern part of British Columbia and that provided me the opportunity to play tour guide. I showed Kelly my old stomping grounds and even introduced her to some old friends we looked up. I'd had no contact with people from my past for the ten years since I had quit drinking. I was curious to see how I would be received.

We had a great time and we discovered that we traveled together well. One of the skills I had learned from my father was how to pack for travel. I was like a wizard in packing everything into the tiny Miata. We both brought five times too much, including a tent and sleeping bags and extra everything. Somehow it worked.

We stayed at great places and savored a wide variety of foods ranging from Russian Dukabor standards in Grand Forks to ribs in Nelson and spaghetti and chicken in the Italian section of Trail. We parasailed in Osoyoos, climbed Red Mountain in Rossland where I used to ski, and skinny-dipped in the glacial waters near Golden. We boated on Kootenay Lake and visited the hot springs of Ainsworth and Radium.

All the while we played a game of pretending where we might settle down if we found a place to nest. Nothing jumped out shouting, "Pick me! This is the place!"

We met with several couples from my past. They all had done well and had nice homes and families. Yet, while there was connection and they were hospitable, I had changed and we were looking for something different, although we didn't know what it was.

We concluded the trip with a new awareness. Thoughts of settling down and getting married had entered the realm of possibilities. We quickly decided that it wasn't yet the time to look at this option. We had work to do on our family connections and needed to develop more intimacy and security in our relationship.

My old car had begun to act up before our holiday. In rapid succession, I had three unplanned visits to local auto mechanics that left each of them about four hundred dollars more affluent. I had just sunk twelve hundred dollars into a thousand dollar car and the problem did not seem to be fixed. The overheating smell that an old engine gets showed no signs of letting up.

We talked about my car problems with my mother when we were playing cards after our return from holidays. The next week she called to ask if we would be interested in her car. She had talked my father into buying a new car and her old one would be available to us. Their car wasn't our style of vehicle, but we were touched by the gesture.

155

One of the teachings I had learned at the Vancouver Attitudinal Healing Center (a branch of the Gerald Jampolsky directed center in Tiburon, California) was that some people liked to give presents as a sign of affection; it honored them to have these gifts received.

We were happy to get reliable transportation. My parents were delighted to be able to extend support to us and they had the excitement of getting a new vehicle for themselves. It seemed like the ideal win-win situation, but secretly Kelly and I didn't like the car. We privately wished that we could find a way to trade it for something we liked without offending my parents.

Within weeks an amazing set of coincidences took place. One evening while we were sitting out on the deck after finishing off an exceptionally tasty barbecue, we were perusing the newspaper movie section to select which show we wanted to attend. We heard a noise that sounded like an old basement window falling shut. I took a quick look around and nothing seemed to be amiss. We showered and changed and went out to the street where mom's gift car was parked in front of the house. The trunk had a deep U-shaped dent where it had just been hit-and-run. I had seen a large landscaping truck leave from across the street and thought that might be the culprit. We reported the incident to the police and the insurance company.

The taillights were intact and the car was drivable. Instead of renting another car, I continued to use the damaged car until I could get an appointment to get it fixed. Two days later, I was stopped in traffic waiting for the light to change at an intersection that angled into my lane of traffic. Suddenly there was a loud bang and my car was pushed forward. A motorist behind me had panicked when a large wasp entered his car; instead of stepping on his brake he had hit the gas pedal. He smashed into the rear of my already crumpled car! After the police responded to the collision I went back to the insurance company. The car was totaled and I had whiplash. As the saying goes, be careful what you wish for – it might come true.

It was time to shop for a different car. There were two problems; I didn't know what I wanted to buy and I didn't have enough job history or collateral to qualify for a second auto loan. In addition, I had to tell my parents what had happened to their car. My mother was sympathetic rather than blaming when I told her about the car. Then I risked rejection and asked her if she would co-sign if I found something I liked. To my surprise and relief, she agreed.

I wasn't really drawn to anything in my price range; the models that I was attracted to were beyond my means. I still had the old car with its overheating problems and it cooperated by not breaking down. We kept looking at cars and our price range kept expanding. Finally, I found a late model, Mazda 626 with all the options except leather interior. I had the car lot install leather and add it to the selling price. This caused some friction with my parents; however they stopped grumbling and consented to co-sign the loan. Kelly and I were happy. A successful sequence of events had transpired and we became owners of two late model vehicles that we both liked.

This was an empowering chain of events. We both felt connected to a higher power and supported by the universe. Kelly had visualized her car and then acquired it at an exceptional price. In like manner, I had undergone a process that provided me with a newer vehicle that I liked. Our financial picture was improving and my relationship with my parents had also progressed a notch.

Then, as so often seemed to be the case in our lives, one more event occurred that had a major impact. The situation in Kelly's group home had steadily deteriorated and reached a point where decisions had to be made. Meetings were held with the tribal agency and the home was closed, the children placed in foster situations and the staff laid off. This was early December and not the best time of the year to lose employment. Kelly was laid-off. Fortunately she had been working there long enough to qualify for unemployment benefits.

It was a mixed blessing. Our money situation was tight but manageable. Instead of her lay-off being a negative and draining experience, it was actually the opposite. Kelly's reaction was relief. She had been freed from a position of pressure, stress and unending frustration. The job had claimed her predecessor's health and had threatened to burn her out in the same manner.

With Kelly's newfound freedom, she regained a lightness in her attitude and began to sing around the house again. I was amazed at her total transformation. Kelly had felt trapped in her occupation and powerless to deal with the complexities of the unyielding system.

This emotional barrage had been coming at her on another level as well. Just before we decided to move in together, Kelly's mom, Ann, had been diagnosed with breast cancer. For the previous year she had undergone chemotherapy, radiation and a partial mastectomy. Further to this, Ann had decided that it was time to end her marriage of over thirty years.

Of course, the change in Kelly's parents' relationship meant that things would be different at her home at Christmas that year. We were given the opportunity to stay at the lake cabin and hoped that we could be somewhat removed from any emotional backlash that might come up. I also was relieved because of the issues I had initiated the previous Christmas when I had a prickly reaction to her family banter.

Over the Christmas holidays, we decided to take our relationship to the next level and announce our wedding engagement. We contacted one of the local native carvers to make Kelly an original, engraved silver band with an inlaid eagle of gold. We planned to have a private celebration at the cabin on Christmas Eve. To my delight, Kelly had the same carver make an identical ring for me. She surprised me with it at our little engagement party.

We made it through the events of the holidays although there was some tension. We never knew for sure if that was directed at me or if it had to do with the separation of Kelly's parents.

We attended a family potluck where approximately one hundred of Kelly's family attended. The food at this gathering was unbelievable. We got through that evening without any social blunders on my part. I maintained a low-key profile and spent a good portion of the time playing with two of my nieces. They were about six years of age and viewed me in that "special uncle" status that required extra attention and a lot of my time.

The new year was soon upon us. After a special ceremony at the lake, Kelly and I returned to the city in a new frame of mind, engaged to be married and wondering what our immediate future held in store for us.

Chapter Ten

Marriage

---

*T*he disco ball ornament that we purchased as a feng shui enhancement reflects dozens of bright spots on our dormant living room walls in an effort to activate the chi energy in the cabin.

The weather is sitting on the fence, toughing out a decision whether or not to generate a few extra calories of heat that would allow us to splash on the oil and begin our annual sun worship ritual.

Last week we had one gorgeous sunny day and our melanin gladly celebrated the event by giving us a preliminary tint of color. It was not quite enough to shift the focus from the extra ten pounds of white flab that we had accumulated over the winter, but enough of a shade to be noticed by others.

I went out to the deck and checked the temperature of the dark green lounger chairs. They were pleasingly warm to the touch. The sun has just inched past the huge cedar tree in front of the cabin and triumphantly indicated the beginning of a choice afternoon. I'll be oiled and on the deck within the hour. The wind chimes are quiet and the billowing white clouds promise to dodge the sun. Having completed my morning walk, I've already roughed out the chapter.

I've just taken my first allergy pill of the season. I haven't had a sneeze attack for at least half an hour but I still need something to take my attention away from my puffy eyes, scratchy throat and wheezing chest. When the pussy willows showed themselves last week, my body took that as the signal to accumulate seasonal irritants in its annual attempt to wreak revenge on me.

It'll be interesting to see how severe this year's bout will be. I believe that the severity of my allergy attacks is directly proportional to my stress level. I hold the same belief about winter colds and flu; it was a relief to make it through the past winter with nothing more than the occasional headache and stuffed nose – my best performance in several years.

Kelly and I have been off work for ten months. Our stress levels are way down compared to the burnout overload of the previous seven years while we worked with kids. The first five months of our sabbatical consisted of a Mexican excursion. For the past five months we've been resting at the lake, writing the book and simply allowing ourselves to be.

Our diet and exercise program has been hit and miss. We've allowed ourselves to have it this way. However, with the probability of family or the general public seeing us in the flesh now, we've recommitted to paying closer detail to our personal self-care plan. We have reintroduced daily walks and are monitoring our food intake once again. Foolishly I had slipped back into the habit of eating butter and ice cream. The constant headaches and extra ten pounds weren't enough of a deterrent for me. Kelly has fared better and for now has a competitive edge as we greet the new season.

I'm amazed at how quickly extra weight piles on. Everything seems to fit the same and then over the course of a short period - like watching the Olympics, for example, there is a major shift. Suddenly nothing looks the same. Waistlines are too snug and shirts no longer hang – they just mold to the contours and by then its almost impossible to become inspired to do anything about it. Nothing fits anymore and none of our clothes look good on us. Even our favorite outfits let us down; they fail to hide the puffy, bloated images we intrusively project onto an unsuspecting world.

The negative self-image and corresponding weight fluctuations are not new to us. These symptoms have lurked in the background of our low self-esteem, ever vigilant and constantly prepared to pounce.

After I had been working with the kids for a couple of years and had begun to live with Kelly, my body had undergone a slow transformation. I had heard that entering a relationship was usually good for a ten-pound weight gain. I considered my work to be a type of relationship. Added to the relationship with Kelly, that meant I should have been twenty pounds heavier. I had slowly allowed my weight to build from one hundred and ninety pounds to something between two hundred and ten and two hundred and twenty. One of my less professional childcare techniques was concluding each session with a trip to McDonald's. Unfortunately, I all too often shared in the treats with my child-clients. As a result, I stoically bore the proof of my commitment.

During this early part of our relationship, while my weight was on the upswing, Kelly was riding the opposite crest. Energized, she maximized her time off and began to eat more healthy foods, diet regularly and release her pent up stress and emotional baggage.

Soon we began to talk of finding a more responsible way of living than spending all of our income on house rentals, especially with the high cost of living that we faced in the city. She was drawn to her childhood roots on Vancouver Island where the cost of living and the pace of life were more in line with our low-key aspirations. She wanted to spend more time with her mother who was battling level three cancer. The threat of loss had brought them closer. Kelly spent a lot of time on the phone with Ann and visited her as frequently as possible.

Kelly missed her two nieces who were the only children of her brother and sister. They were at the cute age of six and seven. Kelly was afraid that they would grow up without knowing her.

As a result, we approached a First Nations agency in Duncan, Kelly's hometown, and made an appointment for an informational interview with the executive director. After a successful introductory meeting, we followed up with resumes and letters of reference.

We had initiated the contact and put out to the universe our intention to relocate to the island and get established. We were good workers and we had good energy. That done, all we could do was trust the process and wait for our higher power and the universe to supply our needs. Spring slipped into summer while we waited for a positive indication that there would be any work for us.

As my annual vacation in August approached, we shifted our focus and energy onto something entirely different. Our thoughts had turned toward getting married.

Neither of us wanted to go through the ordeal of a traditional wedding. With Kelly's large family, we both dreaded the spectacle of a big wedding, which we believed to be too stressful and too expensive. Both of us wanted something simple, preferably outdoors, specifically on a hot, sunny beach. Our first thought was the Oregon Coast. We had never been there but had always heard that it was a place of great beauty.

One year earlier, Kelly's sister had eloped to Nevada and had a small wedding, so the precedent had been set. Kelly was comfortable with the idea of elopement. She further figured that her father would appreciate not being pressured to cover the costs of a large ceremony.

Finally the day arrived for us to elope. We loaded up the Miata and headed south. We had no destination, no itinerary and no particular route in mind. We secondhand shopped along the route to Seattle. There we headed to Pike Place market for pizza and chicken gizzards. Each of these treats from different outlets in the market were regular rewards for us anytime we visited the city. It must be symptomatic of food addiction that we remember places by the culinary treasures we discover.

We then went wedding shopping and found the ultimate coral colored designer dress for Kelly. We had considered a wedding in white but the colored dress looked sensational on her. That accomplished, we drove out to Washington's Long Beach and then proceeded south across the bridge to Astoria, Oregon. To our dismay, the Oregon coast wedding that we had envisioned was impossible. Due to rigid legislation, Oregon didn't have justices of the peace who would perform beach ceremonies. The options in that state were to be married by a minister or a judge indoors. The yellow pages advertised one woman who traveled to perform services but we didn't bother to check it out.

We were very disappointed. Everything had been flowing until suddenly it felt as though we were going against the current. Before pushing on, we stopped at a music store and purchased a copy of Tracey Chapman's sound track *New Beginnings*. That became the sound background for our entire adventure. One of the tracks on the tape was called *Cold Feet*. By the time we arrived at Cannon Beach, Oregon, that name pretty well summed up our attitude toward marriage. Not even the beauty of this seaside resort could prevent us from getting into our stuff. We had plunged from the sublime to the ridiculous. We had gone for our daily walk, in separate directions, and eaten lunch in separate restaurants. Now, back at the car, we argued about who would drive. I insisted it was Kelly's turn – she refused. We sat in that parking lot for three hours and glared at each other.

Fortunately this double tantrum dissipated and we continued our journey south. We loved the beauty of the Oregon coast but we froze. We weren't expecting the dramatic drop in temperature that prevailed along that state's entire coastline. We felt personally responsible for the weather due to the chill that had developed between us.

Northern California continued to be cool along the water but we discovered that it wasn't our fault. With a 30-minute drive inland, temperatures were in the high nineties. Kelly was under the impression that we needed a blood test to get married in California. She was terrified of needles and once again we found ourselves quarreling.

After a delectable chiopanni dish at an old rustic waterfront restaurant we happened on near Fort Bragg, we pushed on to the outskirts of San Francisco. A three state power blackout had rendered an unending string of no vacancies. Through an interminable night of driving, all the hotels and motels were full and all the airports were shut down. Finally, coming into San Francisco at three in the morning, we pitched our two-man tent on the cement pad in a trailer park.

The next morning, we faced a bleary-eyed picnic on the bay in Sausalito and secondhand shopping in San Francisco. That same evening we got lost in San Jose and found ourselves in a scary neighborhood with derelict cars and angry looking teenagers. The next morning we scrammed north out of San Francisco with the intention of getting married in Nevada.

In the realm of free association the name Nevada is synonymous with gambling. With all due respect to the inhabitants of Nevada and to anyone who has been married there, we concurred that we didn't want to start our marriage on a notion of gambling.

We were at a fork in the road. Our options included giving up and going home, getting married in Nevada, or pushing on toward Southern California. Except for layovers at LAX, I had never been in Southern California. For that reason, it was the destination closest to my heart.

We agreed on SoCal. We u-turned that little Miata and headed south once more. Apart from my love of the sun, the Beach Boys and the notion that I would have been a champion surfer if I had been raised in southern California, the other draw, apart from Hollywood, was Salinas. I had long been a Steinbeck fan so our next stop was Monterey.

While we explored the Monterey peninsula, we found a secondhand store in Pacific Grove. After selecting a couple of special things we noticed that we were parked by a new age bookstore. I had the notion that the proprietors could answer our questions about beach marriages.

The owner was quite busy and after waiting awhile for her attention we decided to leave the store. However, the feeling of having missed an opportunity returned and I told Kelly that we should give it one more try. In response to our query, to our surprise the bookstore owner replied, "Well, that's just what I do." Shirley Bradshaw was an ordained minister and informed us that the laws had recently changed. To Kelly's relief, no blood test was required.

We asked if she knew of any good places on the beach for a wedding and she gave us simple directions to an ideal spot, aptly called Lover's Point. Without any further hesitation, we decided to get married August 14, two days hence, at ten in the morning. Not only did it turn out to be a Wednesday, which we thought sounded like "wedding day," but it was exactly six months after Valentine's Day.

The next two days were a busy time, shopping for our bridal suite, getting our marriage license in Salinas, having the Miata detailed and picking up all the odds and ends to make our celebration special. Suddenly we were back in the flow. The day before our wedding, part of the street was closed for an outdoor market. We bought two-dozen white roses for five dollars, received massages on an outdoor table and reserved a honeymoon suite with a four-poster pine bed, tile floors and a balcony overlooking a courtyard garden with waterfalls and a hot tub.

On the eve of our wedding, we had a preliminary ceremony where we each listed all the things that weren't enhancing our lives and that we wanted to release. We then burned the lists on the spot where we were to be married the next day. We asked the universe to cleanse us and prepare us for our spiritual commitment.

At ten the next morning we met the woman from the bookstore at Lover's Point in Pacific Grove. This was our sacred spot. Shirley told us that this was an ancient power vortex for the native people. In fact, the area had once been a battleground, but because of its special energy and beauty, the warring tribes were transformed to peaceful neighbors. It is rumored that it is a site of personal transition and that people performing ceremonies there will undergo a dramatic shift in their lives. They inevitably return from time to time. With each subsequent visit they undergo further spiritual transformation.

Our minister brought everything including a witness who looked like Gilligan from his island, right down to his red sneakers. Gilligan was our photographer and scurried around with the small mice, birds and assorted wildlife that witnessed our ceremony. The minister smudged the area with sage, placed jasmine all around us and cleansed our heart chakras by ringing a huge crystal bowl with a special wand around the rim. As the sun broke through the mid morning mist, Shirley led us in a beautiful ceremony to exchange our vows.

For our wedding feast, she recommended a new restaurant that only the locals knew about. After congratulatory hugs, Kelly and I put a "Just Married" sign on the back of the Miata and headed for our first brunch as husband and wife.

At the restaurant, we met two energetic senior women who sensed our special mood. They were sisters who lived in Pebble Beach. They became our self-appointed hosts and phoned the park commissioner so that we didn't have to pay for the scenic drive to Carmel. It turned out they also loved secondhand shopping and managed a small charity shop that they had patterned after Saks Fifth Avenue. We followed them up to their outlet and went shopping.

We had to backtrack to the restaurant because Kelly had left her purse outdoors in the garden when we posed for pictures. Not to worry, the purse was still sitting right where she had left it. We were grateful and inspired by how easy things are when we were in the flow. We posed for more pictures in Pebble Beach and then at the Old Spanish Mission in Carmel. From there, we went to the beach for more pictures. A ten-year-old boy acted as our photographer and took a series of pictures on the hill and down to the gorgeous white sand of the beach.

Then we returned to Pacific Grove and enjoyed the luxury of our hotel suite before going to dinner in one of the area's better atrium restaurants.

It was a perfect day. We couldn't have planned it better. This showed us how blessed we were, and how well things can go when we surrender to the abundance of the universe and trust the process.

We took our complimentary fruit and cheese basket from the hotel back to Lover's Point and had a special ceremony of gratitude. We read from special angel cards that we had purchased from the bookstore, then fed all the little creatures that came back to see us. It was a magical moment. The spot where we married resembled a medicine wheel with special rock formations all around that added to the spiritual energy we felt.

We returned to the beach at Carmel for a day in the sun before heading on to Big Sur and points south: Santa Barbara, Ventura, Los Angeles, Newport Beach and San Diego. Of course, we took the train to Tijuana and shopped. Then we were homeward bound. We worked our way north up Interstate 5, enjoying the warmth of the inland sun. We side-tripped east to Lake Tahoe, then back home through Portland and Seattle.

Upon our return, we were fortunate to have several days off. On our answering machine we heard the distressing news that my mother had fallen while playing with the dog and had broken her wrist. She needed help with getting the car home from their summer vacation spot. We were a little nervous because we hadn't really prepared either of our parents for the wedding, although we had phoned them on our wedding day. We didn't know if they were hurt for not being included. In spite of our concern, things turned out okay. We celebrated with them and drove my mother home. My father was to follow after completing the necessary departure details.

Kelly and I returned to life in the city, and put energy into the notion of starting our own business. Kelly had been through this before with her former partner so she had experience getting a new business off the ground. We had made a feeble attempt at an earlier idea; however, it wasn't the right thing for us, and our energy soon dissipated. That project had been abandoned.

We both had a passion for secondhand shopping and we had been impressed by the store that the ladies in Pebble Beach had put together. Now we envisioned a similar upscale boutique as something we could create. The more we talked about it, the more plausible it seemed. Kelly enrolled in a one-week course through an education extension program in her hometown on Vancouver Island. This would give her time with her mom who had survived cancer and subsequently made some big changes in her own life.

Kelly returned home with news – some of it not what I wanted to hear. First, the business project had merit and that had motivated Kelly to enroll in a one-month program to put together a business plan and market evaluation. We agreed this was a wise approach that would provide us with all the documentation we would need to make a good proposal to the bank.

The second piece of information was also energizing. Kelly and her mom had begun to look at homes for us and had talked to several contractors. There was a good chance that we could buy a brand new townhouse; the mortgage costs would be about three quarters of what we were currently paying in rent.

Together it looked like we could own our own business and our own home. We would be away from the hectic pace of the city and have the opportunity to begin nesting in a small community near Kelly's family.

Then, there was one more piece of information from her parents that changed my relationship with her family permanently. I had felt distanced from her family since I had spoken out and attempted to set the boundaries around put-downs and put-down humor. In fact I had withdrawn from many of the adults and had joined Kelly in focusing special attention on her nieces who thoroughly enjoyed us. The family was not completely comfortable with the changes that had come over Kelly. She no longer enjoyed social drinking and she seemed to have become overly serious by questioning family dynamics to the point where people weren't completely comfortable. To make things worse she had chosen a partner who did the same thing. We had become a threat to the status quo. To make things worse, I had challenged someone in front of other family members. This news traveled through the family and an anti-Ted alliance had formed.

Another family member had video-taped much of the potluck supper from the preceding Christmas. While viewing the tape, some family members had interpreted that what they had seen of me playing with my niece might be sexually inappropriate. My niece is a Disney fanatic and I had been acting like Pepe Le Peu, the French skunk – mock kissing her hand and arm.

This news tore through the family. Kelly was warned that our wedding should be called off. Kelly's parents were enraged at the accusations and apologetic to us. They let the family know the allegations were untrue. Even the nieces had heard the talk and approached me to express their concern.

However, the damage had been done. The first thing I did was talk to my supervisor at work. A rumor like this would have ended my career in childcare. He listened and supported me. Having known me for two years, he had seen the good work I was doing and how I connected with kids. He helped me process this on a personal level.

Kelly and her parents also supported me. All I could do was allow time to heal the wound. Part of me wanted to retaliate, while another part of me wanted to call the people responsible aside and attempt resolution. Part of me wanted never to return to the Island or see anyone from her family again.

I felt I should share the allegations with my parents. They also supported us as well as possible. Without realizing it initially, I found that I was forming intimacy with my parents for the first time as an adult – the beginning of a relationship with them.

The advice that I got from everybody was to step back and allow the dust to settle. Nothing I could do would help; it would probably make a bad situation worse. There was nothing to cover up. Posturing at defense might inflame the situation. This was not about me – it was about the family members who triangulated and spread the malicious rumor. They had to deal with it. It was their stuff, not mine.

For the first time I really appreciated all the recovery work that I had done and the emotional honesty that Kelly and I consistently maintained in our relationship. I had the ability to detach and hear what people were telling me. I didn't need to react and respond inappropriately. The difference between healthy and dysfunctional responses was becoming more apparent and easier to choose.

In our relationship we processed everything that happened on a daily basis and remained current. There was nothing gunny-sacked that could be thrown back at the other person. Sure we fought, we expressed our feelings, and even did some name-calling, but we never attempted to destroy the other person. We didn't hoard juicy pieces that might sway the balance of power or control. We were equal, and we respected each other.

Now, we had to make the biggest decision of our new marriage. Should we allow the hurtful conjectures to prevent us from pursuing our plans and block us from moving to the Island, or should we simply deal with our feelings and follow our hearts? We decided to look seriously at making the move to the Island in spite of the controversy.

Kelly showed me the units that she and her mother had short listed, and we chose the one that best supported our needs. It was a roomy three-bedroom townhouse. My parents gave us the down payment as a wedding gift and further supported us by co-signing a second mortgage on their home and acted as guarantors. This gave us the money to move our belongings and begin the process of decorating our new home.

My life was changing quickly. Within a couple of months I had eloped, gotten married, made a decision to move and had become a homeowner. We had plans to open a new business sometime in the new year.

Kelly wasn't working and money was tight. If my parents hadn't supported our decision, we wouldn't have been able to afford the mortgage. We were grateful and also felt a little guilty. While we were developing a good relationship with my mother, we were moving further away. This meant that we wouldn't be seeing her as much as in the past. It must have been difficult for her to support us in our move; we knew that she would have liked us to buy a place closer to where she lived.

I kept working in the city on the mainland, which meant that I commuted to work. My job was flexible and I was allowed to set my own schedule. I took the ferry over to Vancouver on Monday mornings and returned home on Thursday evenings. For the first year of our marriage, I was only with Kelly three days a week. The ferry cost me one hundred dollars a week, and I had to spend another hundred on accommodation. I stayed with Peter and Rosemarie, friends who owned the bed and breakfast. It was like being with family. Money had long been one of my core issues and as my financial insecurity reemerged, it created tension that added to the stress of our part-time, distant relationship.

Early in the new year, Kelly attended the month-long business planning course. After analyzing the data we had gathered, the secondhand store wasn't as appealing. The result of our financial plan was negative. It would require too much of our time and the probability of success was marginal at best. There were just too many loose ends that didn't work in our favor. We decided against proceeding and needed to regroup and make a new plan.

I was slowly going into debt and didn't have much of a credit line. To my relief, Kelly took a temporary job with her aunt at a convenience store and gas bar. We were both working, but things weren't working in our best interests. Something had to change. We wondered if we had made a big mistake. We were constantly analyzing every move we made and that increased the pressure. Was this what our higher power had in store for us? Was this our path? Why was it so difficult? Were we following our hearts or were we operating from faulty logic and poor choices?

Things with Kelly's family had quieted down and we were no longer the topic of conversation. Apart from Kelly's parents, only one person came forward and offered us a profound apology, which she extended on behalf of her husband who had been my accuser. Personally, it would have been better received if the husband had come forward but that was not to be. It was a situation where everyone hoped that it would simply go away over time. That old way doesn't work for me – the lack of accountability and personal responsibility.

We settled into a new routine. Kelly had her work and I had my commute. We visited my parents occasionally and had periodic contact with Kelly's family, usually at holidays and birthdays. Life took on the appearance of normalcy.

Try as I could, I couldn't let go of the accusations that had been made. I became aloof with Kelly's family. Another unhealthy dynamic began to surface. I was becoming critical and faultfinding. I listened to the family gossip and paid attention to the subtleties when I was at family gatherings. Slowly, I realized that there was a lot more going on than I initially suspected. There were long term feuds between family members, and some topics weren't openly discussed. Everything from affairs to bad business deals to substance abuse existed within this family. By seeing the family dynamics, I was gaining ammunition to use if the occasion arose. I began to avoid some people, and became careful of what I said and to whom. I didn't like what was happening to me.

It didn't end there. I projected this negativity into my workplace as well. I've never liked working within systems and have always avoided politics. Now I became outspoken and challenged policies and procedures. I avoided many of the workers and isolated myself from them. Later, I realized that this isolation and aloofness had begun soon after Kelly had been laid off. My behavior was finally becoming obvious to me.

I was really frustrated. Kelly and I worked so hard at our relationship and staying clear. Why wasn't this possible any other place in our lives? We knew we couldn't control situations, and we each had our right to our own truth. However, it seemed like no one was doing anything; they wouldn't work through things. All of a sudden the world felt unsafe again. Everywhere I looked it seemed that people were avoiding, distancing or engaging in unhealthy alliances or addictive behavior, alcohol, drugs, eating, shopping sex or busyness.

It was clear that I needed to be spending more time with Kelly in order to remain centered and balanced. We were co-sponsors as well as partners. It was with her that I processed my life and worked my program. I was reluctant to attend AA, ACOA, or CoDA, and I knew that I needed more positive influence in my life.

I was fortunate in that both Rosemarie and Peter at the bed and breakfast had been holistic practitioners and had strong spiritual beliefs that they openly shared. I was able to talk with them about much of what I was experiencing. While our conversations helped me to process, it wasn't completely clear. Rosemarie had also served as a social worker at the tribal agency that now employed me. As a result, we weren't always able to maintain detached impartiality.

I also began to read again, looking for anything that would help my struggling sense of connection and spirituality. The books I turned to were about ascension, awakening and the new order of things. I didn't want to become polarized, however I kept getting the message that there was a new way of being in the world compared to the old, dysfunctional way. I saw myself as expanding and awakening. It was empowering to know that other people were striving to become more than they had been, that they were stretching the limits too, and that it wasn't always easy for them either.

My annual vacation arrived and it was good to spend extra time with Kelly. We had only been together three days a week for almost a year, excluding holidays. Even then we were either with my parents or her family and we didn't really get the time together that we needed.

We celebrated our first wedding anniversary in Vancouver with a special dinner and then to see the Phantom of the Opera. From there we took a quick trip to Washington State and just relaxed together. I knew that our present situation wasn't serving either of us. Since we had made the decision not to undertake the secondhand business we needed to come up with a new plan.

So, after our holiday, I approached a small agency near our home to see if I could do some child care work for them. They were desperate to have experienced male workers and readily agreed. I consented to try some part-time work with them to see how it would go. If everything worked out, I reasoned that I could make a slow transition and leave my work in the city.

To my dismay, it wasn't going to work out. The system couldn't meet my needs. The pay wasn't there, the budget didn't allow for anything near the expenses I had been accustomed to, and the communication with the social workers, when it did happen, was minimal and condescending.

Without my having realized it, my job description and responsibilities at with the current tribal band agency had evolved over the several years of work in Vancouver. I had a great reputation and impeccable references. The outside professionals I worked with referred to me as a therapeutic caseworker and had invited me to sit on planning committees.

I probably could have bitten the bullet and made the slow transition with the new agency in Duncan but my heart just wasn't in it. After my trial week where I had to personally subsidize my outings, one of the kids summed it up, "Thanks for taking us to play pool. I was just happy not to have another worker asking me a bunch of questions and then take me down to the lake to feed the fucking ducks."

There was no flexibility with the new agency and I was greatly relieved to let them know that I couldn't work for them. I chose not to submit a requisition for pay or expenses. I just couldn't go backwards.

Kelly and I were at the place where everything seemed hopeless. There was nothing we could do or think of doing that inspired any action on our part. That was good because it got us to focus on asking our higher power for help. We were slowly approaching our credit limit and were frustrated with my commute. It couldn't continue. We needed something to happen. And it did!

The executive director at the tribal agency where we had done our informational interview a year and a half earlier approached Kelly. She knew Kelly was working at the service station and, after paying for her gas, asked if we were interested in interviewing for a pilot project.

The agency was looking for a live-in couple to provide care for at-risk children in a special care home. These kids were unable to fit into the regular foster care system, and they were faced with a choice between life on the street or time in an institution. She needed an experienced couple that did not have any children of their own. There weren't many suitable candidates to choose from.

We negotiated through the interview process and were hired. We had the option of using our own home or renting a house to serve us as the special care home. The decision was ours. We prepared a proposal, submitted a budget and presented it to chief and council.

The executive director of this tribal agency by-passed our references and directly phoned the director of the agency where we had both worked in Vancouver. This call was made in front of us. As nerve wracking and unusual as that was, we survived the dramatics. We were hired on a contract basis to start in October, the following month.

This left me little time to give official notice and have closure with my clients. Fortunately I worked in association with skilled therapists who facilitated the closure.

To my surprise, my supervisor Walter arranged for me to have a leaving party and the entire staff was invited to it. I asked Kelly to attend with me and this brought up some old issues about her lay off and the closure of the group home where she had been supervisor. I also had reservations about attending because, although I had a working relationship with this group of people, I had alienated from them for some time and didn't feel like a team member.

I was recognized on behalf of the native band chief and counsel as well as on behalf of the agency for the work that I had done with the kids. It was an emotional goodbye. Many of the kids I had worked with attended. Somehow we made it through the luncheon and speeches and good byes. I'm glad Kelly attended because she also achieved the closure that hadn't been forthcoming earlier.

To my surprise, Walter had all my cheques ready for me. Usually it takes weeks or even months to get everything straightened out. There was enough money to clear us from debt and to live on until our contract money began to come in from the new employers.

So another transition was happening. I would no longer have to endure the two-hour ferry sailings on my commute. It had been a difficult year but we had survived. The universe was providing for us. All that we needed had become available in its time, not our time, and we were starting our own business. We were an independent contractor about to meet a challenge. We had absolutely no idea of what we were getting into.

It was an exciting proposition. The money was approximately double what we had been earning before. We would be working with kids and we would be together. We thought at the time that together we could handle anything. We were about to face the biggest challenge of our lives.

Chapter Eleven

Career

I sat down to write this chapter during our last snowstorm of the season. That was the end of March, just prior to Easter. The snow fell so hard that I couldn't see across the lake. The trees were muted images lining the opposite shore.

The television networks had focused on the six-month anniversary of the September 11 World Trade Center disaster. One feature was about the heroic efforts of survivor Lauren Manning, the burn victim who had been fireballed while standing near one of the elevators. Her tenacity and dedication to her recovery were inspiring.

Feeling the pressure of my self-imposed Easter deadline, I rushed through the chronological events of this chapter, not realizing the impact that its content would have on me. The preceding chapters had taken an emotional toll on my fragile serenity and I was prepared to process the residual energy of this current piece in much the same manner over the following few days. I planned to celebrate Easter with friends and family, and then move on to the concluding chapter of the book.

Instead, I found myself slowly shutting down. Like a helpless victim, I watched my self-esteem, confidence and sense of well being melt as quickly as that late season snowstorm. I was left angry, silent, sullen, cranky and frustrated. My emotional hangover completely dried up my creativity. I was not only facing writer's block, I was into borderline depression.

Suddenly, I felt that everything I had written was of no value and that my effort to relate my recovery story was better suited for the trash dumpster in the alley behind some vanity press building. Comparing my life to normal people, I came up short on every account. I no longer thought of myself as an aspiring writer but had to admit that I was an unemployed, aging baby boomer with no retirement package and little hope of ever being gainfully employed.

How could that shift in perception happen so quickly? I needed to be able to create self-employment because I was too fragile to be a team player, too sensitive to other peoples' opinions of me, too self-critical to live up to my own lofty standards.

Then the money issues reared up. Last year I had money in the bank and a hefty monthly salary. Now I was unemployed and my credit card debt was multiplying out of control. It seemed like only a matter of time before I was going to take a big fall and all the king's horses and all the king's men could never put me back together again.

I felt like I had been dishonest with my father who had advanced me the money from my mother's estate. Instead of using it in a prudent manner, I had squandered it on an impulsive need for immediate gratification. I burned with shame and cowered under the lash of his unspoken words. His contempt was so deeply etched into my internal essence that it no longer needed to be voiced. It was always there; I was powerless against it.

Over the winter my healthy eating program had slowly deteriorated. The late evening snacking had once again emerged into our living room. The dairy demons, butter and ice cream, had also regained their hold and slowly I had begun to put on the extra pounds. The clothing I put away last fall no longer fit the loose, comfortable casual look I had enjoyed.

The image of Lauren Manning remained with me and I knew that it was time for me to recommit to my recovery process. Somewhere I remembered that where intention goes, energy flows. It was time to put the book on hold and get back to basics. First things first. One day at a time.

First, I needed to reaffirm ourselves and my decisions. I had to get out of my victim position and validate my choices. This was relatively easy – I needed only to examine the reasons for my decision and return to the place of acceptance that I had earlier chiseled out for myself.

Next, I needed to continue my daily exercise routine and initiate a balanced eating plan. Fortunately, our friends John and Doris are into exercise and good food. They suggested one of the heart diets, which provided plenty of food with little or no fat. As I practiced the diet, pounds began to melt off.

The season shifted, the clocks were set ahead, and we enjoyed our extended evening daylight. Soon we were walking twice a day again. In addition we enrolled in a class of applied somatics that was conducted by a certified Hanna Somatic educator. The gentle movements and stretches quickly improved our posture and flexibility. I began doing an hour of somatics before each morning walk.

We talked about our recent experiences and began the emotional closure that we hadn't completed as yet. We examined our game plan – to take a one-year sabbatical to regain our health. We were right on track. The first five months had been the adventure, journey and busy travel time through Mexico. The second seven months had been the rest and relaxation phase that also included the gentle approach to writing this book.

We continued to listen to our spiritual tapes and even did a reading from our large set of angel cards, which indicated that we were exactly where we were supposed to be. We renewed our resolve to align with our higher power and focus on repelling our fear, negativity, limited beliefs and short supply thinking. We soon saw that our thought process had created our dilemma; the chaos and drama was only a symptom of that unclear thinking process. We were focusing on the past and the future. Instead we needed to return to the present, trust our higher power, and trust the process.

Slowly, over a period of a month, we regained our sense of balance and centeredness. I had lost the extra weight, felt more alive and clear, and was beginning to feel good about myself once again.

Although writing chapter Ten negatively impacted Kelly, she hadn't slipped as deeply into despair as I had. In fact, it was probably more draining to her to be my support as I dug myself out. However, because she chose to participate in the process, she reaped the benefits along with me.

In the past month spring has sprung and the view outside our window is much softer. The subtle shades of green and the April showers are in the process of yielding to the warmth and sun of May. We both are regaining our summer color and have spent good hours sitting back on the deck, reading and playing backgammon.

The other day, I attempted to read the first draft of chapter eleven; I quit half way through. I just didn't like it. Redoing the entire chapter

seemed to be the only viable course. However, it's time to press on to the
sequence of events that weighed so heavily upon us.

Something hadn't felt right when we signed our contract with the tribal agency. The money was ideal, the opportunity looked good, and our energy was high. It was what we wanted – having our own independent business, and contracting our skills out, working with kids. Yet, something was off – things weren't what they seemed.

The first impact on our situation was a tragic accident. The psychologist who was to supervise us was killed in an automobile accident. This meant that, instead of debriefing with a skilled therapist, we were assigned to meet with the child placement resource officer. Not only was that something of a conflict of interest, it meant that we were debriefing with someone who was not trained to hear us clearly.

The second profound impact derived from a decision made by the executive director. She decided to take a six-month maternity leave while she adopted a baby. This put us under the mandate of her assistant who had a different agenda from what we had developed through our pre-employment interviews with the director.

Boiled down, we were starting our new venture without the support or structure that we had expected. Nevertheless, green as we were to managing a Special Care Home, we had strong skills and the motivation to make it work.

Instead of taking some difficult older male teens, we juggled our preliminary placements. That instigated our first conflict with management. I didn't like the decisions that were being made without our input and I let the assistant director know that.

That Christmas came and went, as did our first few months. We had an unusual grouping of three adolescent teenage girls. Although their individual contexts placed them in conflict, we managed to hold it together.

Reportedly, the social workers were awed by our accomplishments and there was talk of our one-year contract being extended. Instead of this being good news, it raised my fear-based thinking. Until now I had no doubt that our contract would be extended. We were good at what we did and had confidence in our success. Now a tiny crack appeared in my confidence; I began to worry what would happen if our contract wasn't renewed. How would we pay our mortgage?

Our honeymoon period with the kids in our charge had run its course. Still things were, for the most part, quite good in our home. There were the expected problems with drugs, alcohol, boys and truancy from school but overall things were working. Because there was more stuff between the kids than with us, we found ourselves doing a lot of conflict resolution.

Conflict arose between the teens in our home and they ran (A.W.O.L.E.D.). We found ourselves in a new situation with no kids in the home. Our contract was half over so we used this natural break to take some much needed respite time.

We gifted ourselves with a two-week respite vacation on Maui. The time went so quickly that we discovered two weeks just wasn't adequate to release all of the accumulated stress and tension. We alternated between downtime and bickering. After about nine days on Maui, we had a major fight. It seemed we needed to do that to release all of our internalized stuff. Then after only a couple of days of real holidays, it was already time to return home – to re-enter the chaos.

Our fight had been a good thing because it moved us to a new level in our money management. Prior to our trip we had maintained separate bank accounts and we shared our costs. As a result of the conflict, we resolved to set up a new format for our banking. This had us pool our money and set up separate accounts for mortgage, household and credit cards. In that way, we returned from our holiday as more of a team.

Unfortunately, but not surprisingly, as soon as we returned our stress level was as high as when we left. This pattern was to repeat itself over and over. We were often reluctant to take our needed respite because it was so difficult to find people who could be trusted to take over our home. Usually the kids would react in the same manner as if they had a substitute teacher - all hell would break loose and we would return to a disaster. Anticipating the mess we would find on our return made us wary of leaving. That in itself was very stressful.

Although the tribal agency had not retained another full time psychologist, they hired Deborah, a part time therapist. We managed to get an hour or so with her every two weeks to discuss the issues in and around managing the home. There was not enough time to debrief our personal stuff.

Things had changed for us at the agency after the conflicts in our home. We were no longer seen in the favorable light that we had enjoyed in the beginning. Further to this, we gave too much detail to the resource officer and the social workers. They didn't want to hear all the stuff we were saying; they just wanted to know whether the mechanics of the household were running okay or not. When we debriefed with them, it created more work for them and they were already overworked. Their caseloads were staggering and they didn't need us adding to that.

The work and the issues were tough. We were attending trials at all levels from shoplifting to murder. The extended families of the kids in our house were in chaos. Alcohol and drugs were ever present in the families of origin, as were incidents of physical, emotional and sexual abuse. The kids themselves faced enormous handicaps from the combination of fetal alcohol syndrome and its effects, not to mention the posttraumatic stress symptoms of the abuse.

As our year ended out, we had seen a steady parade of kids through our home. The combination of issues, and the fact that many of the kids were related and their family histories were intermingled, posed additional conflict and problems.

Several times we came close to a good mix of kids, then external decisions or influences would change the dynamics and things would spin out of control. For example, after a short period of stability, an actively drinking teen would be placed with younger kids. This upset everyone because of the horrors they had experienced in their own homes as a result of drinking. The home would become unsafe for the kids and unstable.

Through all of this, we tolerated kids trying to steal our stereos, a kid who carried a meat cleaver for protection, the violence, intimidation and threats toward the other kids and toward ourselves. All of this slowly began to take its toll. We got a taste of vicarious trauma and found ourselves constantly on the edge. Sudden noises or loud music began to startle us – we became hyper-alert.

After the first year, when it came time to re-negotiate our contract, we were only offered a six-month extension. Although there was relief in having our work extended, the unstated message was that we weren't doing a good enough job. I took this very hard. There was a part of me that wanted to point a finger at the tribal agency and say that a good portion of our problems came from their own mismanagement and lack of support.

We realized that our grumbling indicated a deeper problem. We were undergoing a shift in consciousness resulting from the beginning stages of burnout.

We took a three-week break and flew to Mexico for sun and rest. Like our previous break six months earlier, during the first part of the holiday we were absorbed in bickering and then had a major blow out fight. Finally we had some actual downtime to enjoy and renew ourselves. Upon our return, our stress level was right back to the danger level – as high as it had been before we left.

We resolved to take more small breaks and get away for four-day respites once a month. In the previous year we had taken occasional long weekends when we had traveled to Vancouver or Seattle or out to my parents house for dinner and an evening of cards with my mother. We continued these long weekends and alternated them with four-day respite breaks at some of the nice resorts on Vancouver Island where we could enjoy good food, walk in nature and spend quiet time together.

Still, the stresses began to emerge in other ways. We found ourselves in conflict with one of our neighbors. They played their music so loudly that we could sing along with it in our own living room. Kelly warned me not to get into it with them, but I finally reached a point where I could no longer tolerate it. The woman played her music as loud as her teenage daughter. As our conflict escalated, the bylaw enforcement officer and then the police became involved. Another neighbor was drawn into the mess.

This was nothing new to the kids in our home. They had seen much worse their entire lives. For most of them, violence was the logical conclusion to this type of drama. We attempted to show them a new way to deal with the trouble from next door.

Things with the neighbor progressively degenerated. The man threatened to kill me, and then his wife went to our employers and told them we were abusing the kids in our charge. Fortunately, the agency knew better, but the intensity of the situation fed our ballooning stress level.

As the six-month extension came to an end, we were offered another six-month extension with reduced pay. We were no longer entitled to see the therapist for debriefing. The only reason we were offered the extension this time was because we had a particularly difficult adolescent male somewhat stabilized. The reduction in salary, support and status was another blow to my self-esteem that I took personally.

To add to the stress, two months earlier my mother had been diagnosed with cancer. It was a late stage diagnosis. She had been incorrectly diagnosed and treated for sciatic nerve problems for two years. When the cancer was found, it was too advanced for effective treatment. She began chemotherapy and radiation in February. By summer, she weighed less than a hundred pounds and no longer wanted to eat. There was a brief period in July when she seemed better and was allowed to go home. We visited her then but didn't stay long because it was such a difficult visit.

Six months earlier I had turned fifty years old. On my birthday, it had been my mother's intention to buy me a computer. Both Kelly and I are technically challenged and have no desire to become computer literate. Regardless, my mother tried to force us to take a cheque to buy a computer but we refused. Looking back I wish we had taken the money. It would have honored her.

Nature has a way of leveling things out. Shortly after our contract was renegotiated for the second six-month extension, the problem child's inappropriate behaviors escalated and he threatened Kelly. Having had enough of him, I put him out of the house, packed his bags and delivered them to the social worker. While doing this, I knew that no further extensions would be offered. We had only one teen remaining in the house for the summer and fall. He was a soft kid who had become mixed up with a tough gang. He flourished in our home because he wanted to be there. It made the difficult time of my mother's illness much easier.

In August, my mother fell at home and broke her hip. She was readmitted to the hospital and we began to take the ferry to the mainland on a weekly basis to spend time with her. She stopped eating and was basically starving to death. In mid September, we did what we could to have closure with her. Then the specialist requested to speak to my father and me. It was coming down to the end. We were advised that my mother was entering her last few days. She wasn't in too much pain. In fact, she was feeling somewhat light and elated, a common symptom in the final stages of starving to death.

Kelly and I returned to the hospital to spend the last few hours with my mother. The nurses let us set up a mattress in her room. We lit candles and played soothing music for her. We finally napped about eleven p.m. When I awoke about thirty minutes later to swab her mouth with water, she was cold. It was like she had waited for us to go to sleep so she could die. My mother was like that. She had insisted she would not lose her hair; although she had extensive chemo and radiation she still had thick hair when she passed on.

Within a month after my mother's death, our contract expired. We faced major losses on two levels - the passing of my mother and the end of our employment. We were burned out and exhausted. The natural ebb and flow of life protected us while we started our grieving process.

The director and the resource officer asked us out to a luncheon and gave us a going away card and crested blanket as a token of their appreciation. We had the card mounted and framed. It seemed to ease that part of our sorrow and we accepted it as a peace offering.

We still maintained a relationship with Deborah, the therapist who had been seeing us for the previous two years. She had been conducting our sessions in our home and she was very helpful in guiding us through our grieving process. One of the things that she helped us deal with was our feeling of loss of our good name and sense of worth. She confirmed that she saw us operating with a consistent level of integrity and that we did exceptional work with many of the children who had come through our home. She insisted that our work was recognized by the children and their families. Despite their obvious dysfunctions, they respected us. These children were our true barometers. The kids that had been in our home later greeted us with enthusiasm; they came to us for a hug or a few precious moments where they could share their latest exploits with us.

By the beginning of December, we had put stage one of our grief behind us. We considered re-entering the job market. We had sent out cover letters to a number of agencies and received several promising replies including two invitations to negotiate something. These agencies were on the mainland where there was a high demand for people with our combination of experience and education. It meant that we would have to put our home up for sale and leave the calm island environment.

We weren't sure what to do and went for a drive in the country. On the way home, we asked our higher power to give us a recognizable indication of the path we should take. We were confused, unclear and somewhat afraid of financial insecurity. The move would mean that Kelly would no longer be near her family and would miss the time she spent with her mother.

When we returned home there was a message on our answering machine. It was the resource officer from the tribal agency advising us that one of the sixteen-year-old teens we had previously cared for had given birth to a son. They needed a short-term placement. Could we help them out?

Christmas came and passed and in January the agency asked us if we could commit to a long-term open-ended agreement to care for the mother and child. We agreed on the basis that the mother would follow the house rules, attend school and take an active role as a parent. We set a boundary that we would not parent the baby, but would do everything we could to support the teen to be the best parent she could be.

This pleased all parties concerned and we now had our business operating again. The teen was motivated and things fell into place. There were minor difficulties but they were dealt with as they came up and the months passed. The school had an adjoining nursery and, all in all, everyone was pleased. We had noticed mood swings and shifts in attitude when she had visited her extended family. As we suspected that she was drinking with the extended family, we limited their access to her. As the school year came to an end, that policy proved to be successful.

That summer there were more incidents that indicated drinking. When we took time off so she could have an extended family visit, we returned to find out that the teen had been in jail and the baby placed in care.

As before, the stress was starting to build. We faced escalating problems whenever the teens were outside our umbrella of care.

School started again and things seemed to be getting back on track. The young mother was having problems at school and things weren't going as well as the previous year. However, the baby loved the nursery and got lots of positive attention. A different aunt was now in the picture and there were telltale attitude shifts after each visit.

By October, we were approached by the agency to take back another female teen. This fourteen-year-old had lived with us previously. We consented, subject to the approval by the teen mother. She readily agreed and indicated that it would be nice to have another teen in the house.

Things didn't work out as well as hoped. The two girls began a competition for our attention. The new teen required a lot of work to get on board. Things looked okay but there was some tension and a lot of meetings around the table in order to deal with conflict. Our stress levels began to spike off the scale and we approached the burnout level.

Kelly had heard of a study that seemed to fit our life. An experiment on stress was conducted with two affectionate, playful kittens. They were placed in a cage with an electrically wired floor. The kittens were subjected to random charges of electricity. Over time the kittens began to fight and became increasingly hostile. They reached a point where their stress got so high they began to attack each other and it seemed that they were prepared to fight to the death.

That's what was happening in our lives. Everything looked okay. The social workers were happy and the agency was pleased. The schools were noticing some problems with the girls but they were content to have the teens attend as long as they were under our care.

We weren't doing well. We never fought in front of the kids but there were times when we needed a lot of space. We had our system down to the point where we had a date night every Thursday when we went out to dinner and a movie. Often we spent the largest part of the evening yelling at each other.

Tension began to come out between the girls. That escalated to phone calls from the schools and accusations of shoplifting. Then the issues with inappropriate sexuality came in, and obvious drinking incidents.

We made it through Christmas and into the new year. The older teen and baby wanted out-of-town visits on weekends to visit their aunt. Although we permitted this, the shifts in attitude became more pronounced. Then one weekend she didn't come back.

We took a hard line policy and refused to readmit her to our home unless she recommitted to our original agreement. She would have to attend school, follow the house rules and be a good parent. She chose not to return.

By the end of April, the other teen had returned to her extended family and we were once again without a contract. We were grateful to be unemployed.

In the previous fall and winter, we had considered several longer-term options. This was before the younger teen had moved in and the placement had started to deteriorate. We had looked at our finances and decided that we needed an extra teen to make things work out financially. Things had seemed to be going fairly well with the teen and baby so we rationalized that we could sell our house and buy a larger home where we could bring in another teen mom and baby. The theory was that the older teen could help out the younger and we could prepare both of them for independent living.

We had our nagging doubts; however, and although we were preapproved for a mortgage on a larger home we asked our higher power that if the new home wasn't in our best interest that the purchase be blocked. And as the situation with the teen mom and the other girl unfolded, the process came to a halt.

Another option that we had considered was finding something entirely different to do. Our emotional health was suffering and we were in the last stages of burnout. Our friends, Peter and Rosemarie had managed a bed and breakfast for several years and we considered that as something we could do.

We needed time off and wanted to share an adventure. As a result, we decided to rent out our fully furnished home and take a one-year sabbatical. We planned to buy an old Jeep and drive it around Mexico. We would explore the coastline and spend time on the Caribbean side. We made Cancun our destination. We also thought that we'd look out for the perfect small town with the perfect beach, and the perfect house. We planned to set up as a bed and breakfast, perhaps not just now, but in the future.

The previous five years had taken its toll on our relationship and on our bodies. We had both gained a lot of weight through our habit of medicating our feelings with food. The stress had brought us to the point of quarreling and constant fighting. We looked at the option to sell everything and go our separate ways. If it weren't for Deborah, our therapist, our marriage probably wouldn't have survived. She helped us see that we still loved and respected each other. She reminded us that we had operated a successful business and had favorably impacted a number of children who had been fortunate to come under our care. She also pointed out that we had managed to maintain a high level of integrity and respect and had both excelled at working through our issues. She agreed that we were both emotionally drained and were suffering the effects of extended frontline fatigue and showed signs of vicarious trauma. We needed time to heal. We needed a change of scenery, some adventure and time together, just the two of us. She supported our decision to embark on a Mexican adventure.

Within weeks we purchased a second hand Jeep, had it reconditioned, found tenants who were willing to take over our home and cat, and placed our cars with friends and family.

We planned to drive the coast of Mexico, see all the tourist destinations, and explore to our hearts content. It didn't matter that we didn't speak a word of Spanish and that we had no rigid itinerary. This was the opportunity of a lifetime and we were determined to make the most of it.

Chapter Twelve

Asking For Guidance

I'm sitting outside, writing at the patio table. The old plastic and metal
table rocks each time I move my hand across the page. However, instead
of it being an annoying distraction, I find the gentle rhythm comforting.
Last month I took the table apart and cleaned the mold and accumulated
dirt from the frame and glass top. I secured it with new bolts and lock
nuts. I now have a history with this table. For a mechanically challenged
person like me, a boyish pride emerges – the personal recognition of a job
well done.

I like this feeling – the sense of pride that I so desperately want to
claim for my recovery process and choices that I'm making in my daily life.
It too often eludes me. For the past month and a half I have experienced
writer's block, a veil that keeps me stuck in a place where I no longer
wish to be. I'm not sure if it's old stuff about my past, more recent feelings
about the futility I experienced working with the kids, or if it's the fear of
failure or the fear of success about writing this book. I've been wallowing
in that place far too long. I feel dread at bedtime and resistance to sit
down and write every morning. Guilt gnaws at me constantly.

The sun is shining and if the clouds stay away it will likely get quite
warm today. This is the first time that I've tried writing outside and I'm
happy to be sitting here, taking the sun, wearing only my shorts. Out on
the lake, the neighbor has just maneuvered his ultra-lite floatplane into
position for take-off. A ski boat with its driver, spotter and a skier in a
wetsuit have paused from their slalom course passes to allow the ultra-lite
room to navigate. I feel connected to them.

189

They are unaware of me sitting here putting words on paper. Yet we are sharing this moment in the sun at the lake, each in our own way. As the ultra-lite completes a burst of speed and rises into the air, the ski boat and water skier resume their passes.

My role as observer ends and I continue working, busy at my table. It dawns on me that we are each pursuing our own passion in this moment and each of us derives a unique sense of fulfillment and happiness. I do not want this to be a fleeting moment, assigned to days off or recreational activities. I want my life to be filled with passion and purpose. I want that to define how I am in the world and how I earn my living.

This week marks the one-year anniversary of beginning our healing sabbatical. We are feeling much better. The time has passed quickly. On our walk this morning I talked with Kelly about my inability to write. She let me know that it didn't matter if this writing ever got published or not. What mattered is that we took a risk and did something that we both wanted to do.

The preparation for the trip last year was an important beginning for the deeper aspect of our journey: challenging our belief systems and deciding to follow our hearts.

When we put our home up for rent, we initially talked to the manager of a local property rental company. He told us the figure that we had in mind was out of line – we couldn't possibly cover our mortgage payments by a monthly rental. He concluded that if we added his management fee and the storage rental for our furniture, we would only lose about four hundred dollars per month. We politely left his office and threw his forms and advice into the nearest garbage can.

Then we drove to the local newspaper office where we placed an advertisement for our townhouse, completely furnished. Within three weeks we had a young couple that was happy to rent our place. They indicated that if they could raise the down payment they might wish to purchase the home if we would consider selling. They even agreed to baby-sit our cat, Bannister.

The other major pre-trip decision had to do with which vehicle we would take. Kelly's Miata had worked for our short trip south when we had married, but wasn't large enough for an extended trip. My sedan had a sunroof but didn't offer the freedom and fun that we sought. So we located a thirteen-year-old Jeep Sahara and had it mechanically updated. We removed the back seat and installed a locking aluminum travel box that we had custom built to hold our luggage.

Before heading south we spent a few days in Vancouver at our friend's bed and breakfast. This interlude was just long enough to remind us how we used food to medicate our feelings, ritualize our daily routines and satiate our need for comfort and fulfillment. As the denial around our eating disorder lifted, we recognized how overweight we had become.

We bid adieu to our friends, to half eaten cartons of Cherry Garcia and coffee Haagen Daz and headed south. Our first stops in Washington State were our favorite discount shopping stores. We apathetically tried on bathing suits, unable to see beyond our need to lose weight. That day we began our healthier approach to eating - diet bars, bottles of water, veggie wraps and low fat meals.

We blew out the stereo speakers listening to the Beach Boys as we entered northern California. By Memorial Day weekend we had worked our way south to Salinas where we obtained copies of our wedding license. We had read that it was important to be well documented while driving in Mexico and we weren't taking any chances. Of course, we spent a few glorious days in Carmel eating delicious food and basking in the sun. We wished we had the financial resources to spend several months or years hanging out here, but this journey lay south of the next border.

Our next stop-off was the Grand Canyon. We drove, top down with no air conditioning through the Mojave Desert. I loved the sun but Kelly was more cautious. We burned enough to shed the skin formerly known as our foreheads and noses.

Between the Grand Canyon and Sedona we became accustomed to the heat. Our friends in Sedona weren't home so we pressed on to Phoenix. There we hit an Arizona style heat wave. After several days of shopping, we drove to Tucson where we got travel visas and automobile insurance for Mexico. We had intended to drive through Texas and cruise down the Gulf side of Mexico to Cancun. But the heat was so intense that, when we learned that we could reach the western beaches of Mexico in one day, we made a quick decision. Enough heat! We wanted beach and water. Heading south to Rocky Point – Puerto Peñasco on your map – we began our circumnavigation of Mexico.

We drove the entire coast south, spending several weeks each in Puerto Peñasco, Mazatlan, Manzanillo, Acapulco, Puerto Escondido. Then we crossed the Isthmus of the Yucatan and worked our way to the Caribbean side passing through Chetumal and arriving at Playa del Carmen. We preferred this smaller Caribbean resort and decided to stay there instead of the busier and pricier Cancun.

There was so much to our trip that I can't even begin to describe it here, nor is that the purpose of this book. We didn't include Puerto Vallarta among the places we stayed. We had spent three weeks there a couple of years earlier and didn't feel the need to repeat. We did check out Ritto's Bacci on the way through Puerto Vallarta. On our last visit we had given him several pasta recipes. Now we discovered that, true to his word, he had listed Pasta Kelly on his menu; Ritto said it was one of his better sellers.

We loved the sun, the beaches and the adventure of traveling. We negotiated for almost everything. Although we knew virtually no Spanish, we never really had a problem communicating with the people. What we didn't find was the quaint little village that we would fall in love with and where we would purchase a large enough house to operate a bed and breakfast. There were lots of nice spots, but that certain one just didn't come to us. We supposed that it just wasn't meant to be. We talked to many helpful people who were operating places or owned businesses and got some good ideas, but we just didn't find a place where we fit. We didn't have the cash to see it through, had it appeared, and our level of residual stress and anxiety probably blinded us to many opportunities.

Apart from the beaches and water of the Caribbean, the place that we were most attracted to was the surfing hot spot, Puerto Escondido. But, like so much of the coastline, the water was too treacherous for our taste. The Zicatela where the surfers ride the pipeline was a deadly stretch of water. The riptides and pounding surf were more than we bargained for. Most of the other resorts were overcrowded or not as clean as we had hoped.

By the time we had reached Playa del Carmen we were becoming somewhat disheartened. On one hand we were excited to be staying on the beautiful white sandy beaches with the clear, warm, calm, turquoise water, but we were not at ease about our future plans.

In our daily meditations we had consistently asked our higher power for guidance and to reveal our next step to us. We were beginning to get frustrated and my faith was bottoming out. Now several months into our journey, our money was running low, and we still had no concept of what our future would bring us.

One couple we met from Canada had created a thriving business with a restaurant, bakery and rental units; another couple had become part of a futuristic jungle commune, which aspired to be a healing center. Each of them had followed the path of their passion and created something. Others we met owned nice homes and villas, which they rented out. None of these opportunities resembled our dreams.

Then one day, while walking the beach in Playa del Carmen, we hit upon the notion of writing a book. The change in our energy was conspicuous. It was something we thought we could do! Several topics came to mind: relationships in recovery; working with kids; our journey of recovery. The more we thought about it, the more the energy grew. It was a different energy than anything that we had ever experienced.

Neither of us had ever thought of ourselves as passionate about writing. Our passions centered around other things: food, beaches, the sun, shopping, time with friends, travel and adventure. We were also both very intense and passionate about our recovery and the effort that we had put into our respective processes. Kelly was verbally articulate and I had some writing skills to express myself clearly on paper.

We shared our idea with several people and then simply let it rest. We focused on the daily concerns of our depleting money, mulling over how soon we should head back to Canada. The notion to write shifted to the back burner and then to a remote place at the back of our minds.

We left the Caribbean at the end of August and thought that we might spend a couple of weeks along the Gulf Coast if we found a great spot. Although we enjoyed the drive and the historic sites and towns, we had been spoiled by the spectacular coastline of Quintana Roo. Apart from brief stopovers in Campeche and Vera Cruz, we progressed toward Texas and points north.

Our bittersweet last glimpse of Mexico on that last night found us in Ciudad Victoria near the Texas border town of Brownsville. I was disappointed to be leaving Mexico and would have liked to return to the Caribbean for another month. I wasn't looking forward to getting home; I dreaded facing going back to work.

I had been avoiding negative thoughts and nagging fears that every so often threatened to knock me off my holiday perch. Instead, I was able to say that we had successfully circumnavigated Mexico with only one minor incident – someone had smashed our windshield in Puerto Escondido.

That last evening, however, my serenity and sense of safety were shattered as we witnessed a brutal incident between police and a couple of angry drunks. One drunk was lashing another with a long belt while the police tried to break them apart. It struck a deep chord in me – echoes of childhood strappings – and I shut down emotionally. This was the end of the first week in September 2001, and foreshadowed the violence we were to witness in the upcoming week.

We experienced a culture shock on our return to the states as we meandered north to El Paso via San Antonio. On September 11, we were having repairs done on our Jeep in El Paso. Strolling through a plaza, we heard of the terrorist attacks. A friend of the station owner took us to a truck stop for some Texas Bar-B-Q where we witnessed the drama playing out on a television propped crudely on a table in the middle of the restaurant. The restaurant was packed, yet strangely subdued as the shocked patrons stared at the broadcast in disbelief and horror. Many cried. We were all changed forever. At that moment we couldn't fathom the full effect of this incident on us.

Our spirits were bruised. For the first time we felt like we were a long way from home. I had never been to New Mexico; I had wanted to visit there for years. However, after the events of September 11, the rest of the trip was a fog. I have some memory of Sante Fe, yet little recollection of Albuquerque. We loved Denver, fought in Vail, and spent the night in Aspen near the base of the ski hill. I vaguely remember Salt Lake City and then Boise, Idaho. It's not like we drove straight home. We did a lot of bargain shopping and found great deals at the discount aisles in our favorite stores. Then we ran straight through Oregon, Seattle and Bellingham, Washington, and back to the Canadian border.

We usually took the truck crossing back into Canada because it was much faster than the Peace Arch route. To our relief, there were no long line-ups. But, to our dismay, there was something at the international crossing that we hadn't seen since the Mexican road blocks – militia with visible guns. To see this at our peaceful border where we had passed from the United States into Canada many times in the past, I was much more nervous than at any of the road blocks where the armed Mexican inquisitors mimicked our English accents. This was serious business between the U.S. and Canada. It put me face-to-face with my fear.

We just wanted to be across the border and back home. But where was home? Our house was rented out and would be for at least two more months. We had been in touch with Kelly's mom, Ann. From her we had learned that my father was raging that we had been away for so long. He had thought that we would be away for only several weeks, not months. Now we felt obliged to visit him on our way home. That old fear from childhood was emerging.

At fifty-two years of age, the fear was as crippling as it was when I was five. I grew up with fear and intimidation; as much as I would like to be beyond it, it still has a tremendous impact on my life. The only redeeming piece of this unhealthy form of power and control is that I am older, have better coping skills and can give myself better choices.

When we visited, after his initial blow up, my father calmed down when we acknowledged his anger and listened as he expressed himself. On a certain level, we knew that he too was afraid and needed to release his fear. It came out relatively cleanly and, after his rant, we took him out for dinner and a visit.

After reconnecting with friends in Vancouver, we returned to Vancouver Island. There we were fortunate to find that Kelly's family lake cabin was available. It was one morning by the lake that we realized that we were now living in the perfect place to write the book we had envisioned in Mexico. The ideas took form and we committed to the project.

Months earlier at the beginning of our trip, we knew that we had been doing front-line work for too long and had reached a point of burnout. We had both gained a lot of weight and our unhealthy eating patterns had reached the level of food addiction.

We had been constantly operating at maximum stress and routine daily events put us over the edge. We were angry and reactive. We didn't trust the universe and what it had in store for us. We were completely in opposition to the tribal agency (our client) and we were caught up in power and control issues. We needed complete control of our daily lives to feel safe. Our fear of financial insecurity distorted our sense of reality.

Under that umbrella of tribal employment, we had begun to bicker and fight; it became a constant state of siege between us. There had been the constant threat of losing our home because the basis of our income was contractual and it never seemed safe or secure. It felt like we had no empowerment in our life. Instead, our destiny was in the hands of other people.

At that time we hadn't had an alternative solution and we were too burned out to begin something new. We sensed that we wanted to remain autonomous but we felt compromised to continue our work. Neither of us had the energy or the peace of mind to create something new. We had talked about divorce, selling our assets and going our separate ways. Yet we knew that we still cared for each other but we were being controlled by the debilitating fear that we had manifested. Logic and spiritual awareness told us that the fear was an illusion – false evidence appearing real – yet it was overpowering.

The first five months of the sabbatical had led us on a wonderful holiday adventure through Mexico that was distracting and set the stage for our healing process. We had to acknowledge that this was the first real time we had spent together in our first five years of marriage. The first year I had been commuting to Vancouver, while the last four years we had kids living in our home.

Our marriage had never really had a chance. We had put career and financial obligations ahead of relationship. It hadn't been our intention to do this; we had merely fallen into the trap of letting appearance and conformity distort our priorities.

Upon our return from Mexico, we recognized that those five months had been about busyness and distraction. We needed time to heal at a deeper level. We cared for each other and we wanted the chance to get healthy while enjoying time together.

The logical question arose, "How could we afford to take more time off?" The answer was that if we wrote a book and managed to sell it, things could be okay.

It was a risk – yet no greater than the risks we had been taking for the past several years. It was just another business decision. We had an excellent credit rating, so we decided to take the risk and finance the balance of our sabbatical on our credit line. It seemed no different than someone attending a buying show, purchasing a large inventory and then establishing a business to sell the inventory for enough profit to earn a living.

We rationalized that most people felt confident in purchasing a new car or truck for somewhere between thirty and fifty thousand dollars and then taking the time to pay it off. Instead of buying a vehicle, we chose to invest in ourselves, in our health and our future. We owned three vehicles and had some equity in our home. We were willing to risk all of that to follow our inner guidance.

Our spiritual guidance suggested that people need to risk putting their asses on the line for God knows what. This is the commitment to trust and faith and ultimately leads to the experience of surrender.

Neither of us had the energy or motivation to find a job so we reasoned that the thing that we could write about was our experience, strength and hope around recovery. Judging from the energy we felt when we talked about the project, it was the best choice available to us.

We live our recovery process; in fact, our close friends are all committed to growth or recovery in one way or another. Our friends all encouraged us to follow our inner guidance. They were so supportive that we felt an obligation to follow this path.

Our tenants at the house asked if they could extend their lease for another year. That set the stage for us to begin the project.

It was an exciting venture for us – a time to nest, rest and, for the first time since I had been advised to do so years earlier, to strive to achieve a boring life.

We settled into a routine where I would attempt to write in the mornings, walk and do errands in the afternoons and read, play cards or backgammon or watch TV in the evenings. It gave Kelly lots of time to talk on the phone and provided her opportunities to be with her mother.

We were midway between two small cities and alternated weekly trips to one or the other to have lunch, go bargain hunting, and to see the occasional movie. We created a life of simple abundance and all our needs were met. We ate healthily, exercised and walked daily. We loved living by the water. The restorative energy of the lake combined with our boring lifestyle impacted us in a healthy way.

People began to ask us if we were on vacation. They commented on how healthy we looked and how we seemed to glow. Surely, this was a better way of living than anything we had done prior.

Slowly we envisioned a new lifestyle for ourselves. We still liked the city and wanted to spend time there as well. We enjoyed walking the sea wall, the restaurants and the energetic hum of the people going about their routines. We also were becoming fond of our new lifestyle and wondered if we should just sell our home and rent instead. This way we could spend time in the city and at the lake. We liked the lifestyle that we had created and identified with it as our new way of being in the world. In fact, we reasoned that we could also travel and maintain this lifestyle - once one or two books had been published. We could write a book in Thailand or in Europe. But enough future tripping – first things first. We had to complete the first book: write it, and then find out how to get edited, published and marketed.

The messages that we were hearing on the talk shows and from our spiritual tapes all seemed to convey the same messages. People needed to discover a sense of self instead of spending their lives working at jobs that they thought they were supposed to be doing to please family or society. It was important to get in touch with what we each really want to do. The messages coincided with our own process. We were slowly gaining clarity on what we wanted to do.

From time to time, fears about our project would emerge. Were we taking too great a risk? Were we burying ourselves in debt? Would it spiral out of control?

Our spiritual teachings and daily meditations reinforced our position and we headed off the unwanted fears, negativity, limitation and scarcity thinking as they showed up. Our ability to practice our recovery tools was improving. Whenever we succumbed to negativity we meditated and talked our way back to clarity and balance. We continued to get exceptional support from our synergistic group. On the whole we remained positive and energized.

Then, about the time of writing chapter eleven, things began to get more difficult. Fears and issues became more current and there was still rawness to some of the feelings of rejection and other issues that lingered for us. We revisited the death of my mother and the sense of failure that we experienced in the relationship with our client tribal agency.

Doubts and fears began to niggle at us and the anxiety and tensions resumed on a small scale. It became difficult to write and I found excuses to procrastinate. The pressure to finish the book then came into view. This set up guilt as I took extended periods of time away from the writing table. The fears of financial insecurity came back into focus and it seemed that we were making poor choices, taking steps backwards and possibly facing bankruptcy. Shame and humility loomed strong.

Part of the fear was about being good enough. Who were we to think that we could function differently and march to a different drummer? Those old messages of "you're too big for your britches" surfaced. The stuff was about never being good enough in the eyes of others. Who would want to read what we had written? Weren't we being presumptuous to assume that anyone would want to publish this stuff?

The old anxiety set in. There's a biochemical change that accompanies this and I swear that I can taste it when it sets in. We were beginning to lose sleep. We knew that the only way to get beyond this fear was to move through it. What did this mean now that we were experiencing the intensity of our situation? The tools seemed suddenly inadequate, the meditations seemed airy-fairy, and the support from our friends seemed more like polite commentary and obligatory gestures. Self-doubt had crept in and was ravishing me.

Fortunately Kelly and I usually slipped into our stuff at different times and we could slowly pull each other out of the depths. There were days when we both slipped in and we needed ultimate space.

The thing that we knew for sure was that if we didn't move through this fear that we would be condemned to live in it for the rest of our lives. The life of quiet despair was not the path we chose for ourselves. Again and again we had to refocus our intention and come back to a level of commitment. Somehow we knew that in order to move through all these fears that we had to see the project through to completion.

We wanted to choose the path of healing, good health, positive energy, passion and creativity. We drew away from the alternative – the life of quiet desperation, the role of victim, always compromising, growing steadily angrier and angrier, growing more and more unhealthy, slipping into addictions, disease and early death.

Then the universe began to send us some curve balls. Our beautiful cat Bannister, the fighter, and the mouser who thought he was a dog, died suddenly. The vet's office said it was either poison or cancer. Our grief began anew.

Then Kelly's dad, Bob, sold his half of the cabin that we rented. We had to be out sometime in July. Our stability was threatened. The new owner said we could continue to rent and that we could return as soon as the seasonal revenue tenant completed his holiday in August - yet we were unsettled.

Then our tenants gave notice on our place - six months earlier than our verbal agreement. The financial threat caused us both to lose several nights sleep. The universe seemed to be telling us that it was time to move along to complete this part of the project, to take care of some business and then refocus. Our financial insecurity had resurfaced and it was difficult not to obsess about debt maintenance and growing interest rates.

The pressure to complete the book became staggering; yet the fear to enter the next phase seemed even harsher. Our credit was running out. We still had no idea of the next phase. Do we need a lawyer or an agent? Could we submit directly to a publisher? Would they reject us? Would we have to return to work?

We had been reading that surrender had to be experienced. It was not something that could be neatly rationalized. It was an emotional event that included anger, rage, rejection and despair. Well, both of us arrived at that place. As the days passed we slowly got our focus back.

The most important thing we could do was to remain in the present. In the present all our needs are met and everything is taken care of. Living in the past or catastrophizing about the future is never helpful. And then, we were fortunate to get the continued support of our small group of friends:

Olga, the woman who taught herself to paint the art of the world's masters and has been pursuing her own path of spiritual growth for many years, continued to give us the message that it was essential to complete the project.

Ann, Kelly's mom, a survivor of level three cancer, had entered a new place of her battle. The edema and frozen right shoulder caused by removed lymph nodes and a fracture due to osteoporosis led her to enter a committed phase of lymphatic drainage and somatic physiotherapy in the hopes of regaining the use of her arm. Her strength inspired us.

Eileen, who has been on her own path of recovery from codependency and sexual abuse is deeply committed to her journey. She has both financially and emotionally given of herself to our works. She believes in us.

And Barb, a single parent who has raised three children on her own, dealt with codependency and panic disorder, started her own business and purchased her own home, volunteered to type the manuscript of the book and do the computer searches for us. She has been a consistent source of support.

How could we not see this project to the end? Initially we were divinely inspired to write the book and more importantly, because of our recovery process, we attracted the support system that spiritually inspired us to see it to completion.

We were also strongly inspired by our neighbors at our townhouse. Doris inspired us to begin somatic exercises and follow a healthy eating plan by providing us with a simple heart smart diet. Her partner John, who recently had his colostomy reversed, had inspired us to remain focused on hope and faith.

We are not sure where our path will lead us. Hopefully, it will be to write another book. We plan to write about moving through the blocks to intimacy and forming committed relationships for people who are in recovery and pursuing a spiritual path. We are spiritual beings having human experiences. As we learn to manage the fears we create, and let go of the veils of illusion, we get closer to experiencing the truth that we are One.

The alternative is no longer a choice. It is impossible to move back into denial. A posture of fear, in a position of victim, is paramount to living a life onset by anger and addictions and that can best be left in the last millennium – in a time long ago – a time of personal powerlessness, characterized by a lack of accountability, better known as a time WHEN YOU'RE NOT YOU!

Kelly and Ted live in Vancouver 's west end near Stanley Park and the seawall. They enjoy spending time together and manifesting a life of simple abundance. Their favorite activities include spending time outdoors, walking the seawall, going to the beach, secondhand shopping, dining in ethnic restaurants, and sunshine.

For more information or to contact the authors please visit us online:

http://www.macadamiapublishing.com

Ted McIntyre & Kelly Dame
Macadamia Publishing
#102-1025 Chilco Street
Vancouver, BC
V6G 2R7

Customer Order Form

DATE:					
Retail price:	$___ (CDN)	$___(USD)	£___	€___	# of copies _____
Book Ordered:	When You're Not You By Ted McIntyre and Kelly Dame ISBN: 1-4120-6624-7 Catalogue Number: 05-1535				
Customer Name:					
Mailing Address:					
	zip/postal code				
Billing Address: (If different than above)					
	zip/postal code				
Phone:		**Email:**			
Visa	**MC**	**Amex**	**Cheque**		
Name on Credit Card					
Card #			**Exp.**		
Select the delivery Method:					
Surface		**Air**			
Please allow:					
2 to 4 weeks for order processing, printing, and shipping via Surface Mail to US and Canadian Addresses					
1 to 2.5 weeks for order processing, printing, and shipping via Airmail.					
Shipping and handling charges will be added. A receipt will be included with your shipment. THANK YOU					

ISBN 141206624-7